I wonder if I can keep up with...

The speed of a world you're not in.

BLEACH 49 The Lost Agent

Shonen Jump Manga

STARS AND

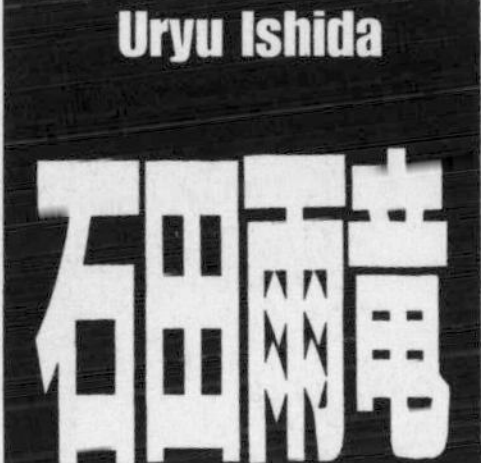

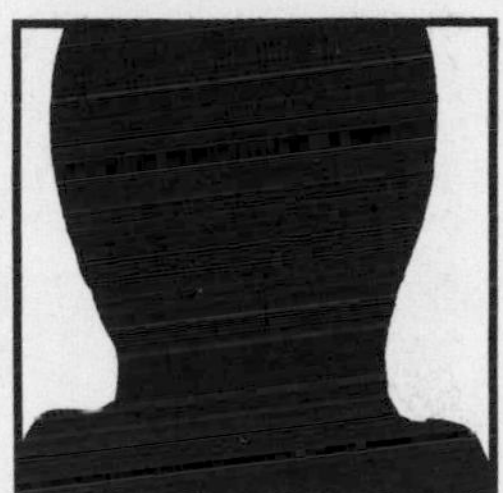

When high school student Ichigo Kurosaki meets Soul Reaper Rukia Kuchiki his life is changed forever. Soon Ichigo is a soul-cleansing Soul Reaper too, and he finds himself having adventures, as well as problems, that he never would have imagined. Later, in the Soul Society, Ichigo stops Rukia's execution but finds out that the entire thing was Aizen's dark plot. Aizen then leads his Arrancar army and declares war on the Soul Society!

As Aizen becomes stronger and stronger, Ichigo continues losing his friends. Ichigo then risks his life to master "the final Getsuga Tensho" and trades his Soul Reaper abilities to finally defeat Aizen. Immediately following, the Hogyoku steals Aizen's powers and the battle ends. Ichigo's powers that saved his town and friends then start to vanish. Is this the last time he'll ever see Rukia…?

BLEACH ALL

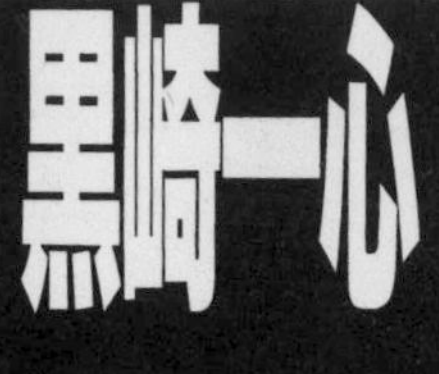

STORIES

BLEACH49
The Lost Agent

Contents

KARAKURA TOWN 7:00 A.M. MONDAY

BROTHERRRR!

IT'S MORNING TIME!!

クロサキ医院

*KUROSAKI CLINIC

424. The Lost Agent

WAKE UUUUUP !!

ICHIGO KUROSAKI: AGE 17

HAIR: ORANGE

EYES: BROWN

OCCUPATION: HIGH SCHOOL STUDENT

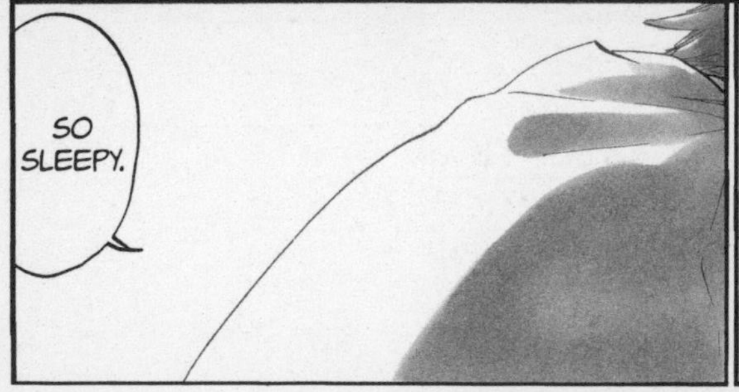
SO SLEEPY.

I CAN'T SEE GHOSTS.

BLEACH
ブリーチ

BLEACH
ブリーチ

READ THIS WAY
TA-DAAAAAA!!
OH.
RIGHT. TODAY'S YOUR SCHOOL'S OPENING CEREMONY.
KARIN.
GET ME SOME SOY SAUCE, WILL YOU?

SLAM

HERE!
YOUR SOY SAUCE!
WHAT'RE YOU SO MAD ABOUT, YUZU?
I'M NOT MAD!

I WAS SO CAREFUL TO NOT SHOW YOU MY SCHOOL UNIFORM UNTIL THE DAY OF THE OPENING CEREMONY AND YOU DON'T EVEN CARE!
WELL, FORGET IT!
I DON'T CARE IF YOU GET THE BURNT PART OF THE RICE!

YOUR ZIPPER'S DOWN.
EEK!

SEE? I WAS LOOKING.
IDIOT!
YOU PERVERTED BROTHER !!
MY GLASSES!
ZOINK
SHATTER

NOTHING.

WHAT IS IT, KARIN?

THUDTHUDTHUDTHUD
YUUUUZUUUUUU!!

PLEASE TAKE A LOOK AT THIS, YUZU!
HOW DO YOU LIKE THE SUIT?
AND SHOULD I GO WITH THE NECK TIE OR THE BOW TIE?!

RIGHT.
LOOKS FINE TO ME.
WHAT-EVER.
WHAT-EVER ?!

IT'S BEEN 17 MONTHS SINCE THE BATTLE. JUST A LITTLE OVER A YEAR.

NOW I'M A SENIOR IN HIGH SCHOOL.

WHILE I WAS ASLEEP, CHAD AND INOUE TOLD EVERYBODY ABOUT THE DEAL WITH MY SOUL REAPER POWERS.
THEY TOLD ME EVERYONE BELIEVED THEM.
THEN AGAIN...
AFTER SEEING WHAT THEY DID WITH THEIR VERY OWN EYES, OF COURSE THEY WOULD.

STILL, I'M GLAD THAT THEY ACCEPTED IT WITHOUT ASKING ANY QUESTIONS.

MORNING.

BUT...
NOW I DON'T HAVE ANY SOUL REAPER POWERS.

ABOUT WHEN I LOST MY POWERS, KARIN'S SPIRITUAL POWERS STARTED GETTING STRONGER.
BRO-THERRRR!!

NOW KARIN'S THE ONE WITH THE DISPOSITION TO BE A HIGH-END MEDIUM.
HAVE A NICE DAY!!

SHE ACTS LIKE IT'S A PAIN IN THE BUTT, BUT SHE HASN'T COME ASKING ME ANY QUES-TIONS.
SO IT SEEMS SHE'S COMING TO TERMS WITH IT PRETTY WELL.

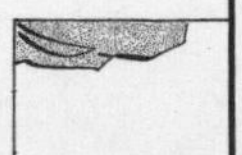

LET'S GO, MIZUIRO.
RIGHT.

KARAKURA 1st HIGH SCHOOL

IIIICHIIIII...
...GOOOO !!

YOOOOOOO!!

CRAAASH
WELL.
I'LL BE ON MY WAY.
RIGHT!
I'LL SEE YOU AGAIN AT LUNCH!
PAT
PAT
PAT
ICHIGO! ICHIGO!!
I'M TAPPING OUT! I'M TAPPING OUT, SEE?!
3-3

ICHI-GO!

DID YOU BRING TEKKEN?

THE NEXT ONE'S COMING OUT SOON, SO I NEED THAT ONE BACK ALREADY.

RIGHT.

I BROUGHT IT. I BROUGHT IT.

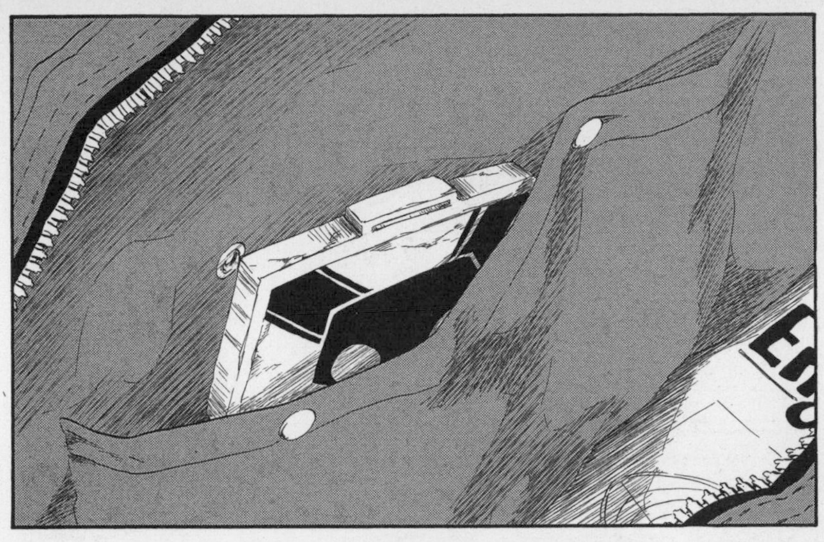

WHAT? DID YOU FORGET IT?
SHOVE
SHUT UP.
I BROUGHT IT, SEE?

THAT REMINDS ME, I FORGOT TO RETURN THE SUBSTITUTE BADGE.

I GUESS THE BADGE STOPPED WORKING AFTER I LOST MY SOUL REAPER POWERS.
AND WITH THE VISIBILITY BARRIER GONE AND THE HOLLOW ALARM NOT RINGING ANYMORE, IT'S JUST A REGULAR PLAQUE NOW. I FORGOT IT WAS EVEN IN MY BAG.

READ THIS WAY

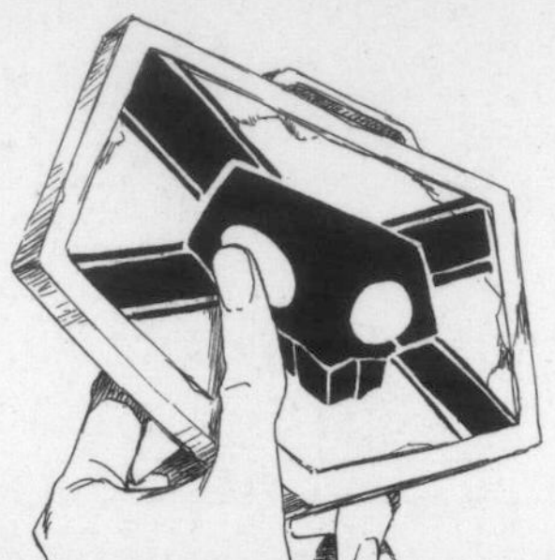
RIGHT NOW, THIS IS THE ONLY...
...PIECE OF EVIDENCE I HAVE...
...THAT I WAS EVER A SOUL REAPER.

HEY!
ISHIDA, WHERE DO YOU THINK YOU'RE GOING?!
TO THE NURSE'S OFFICE!

NOW ISHIDA'S TAKING CARE OF ALL THE HOLLOW EXTERMINATION I DID.
IT'S PROBABLY SOMETHING THAT SHOULD BE LEFT TO IMOYAMA, BUT IT SEEMS HE'S NOT VERY RELIABLE.

THMP
I HOPE HE DOESN'T OVERDO IT AND HAVE THE SOUL SOCIETY GET ON HIS CASE.

EVER SINCE THEN, RUKIA...

...HASN'T COME TO KARAKURA TOWN ONCE.

READ
THIS
WAY

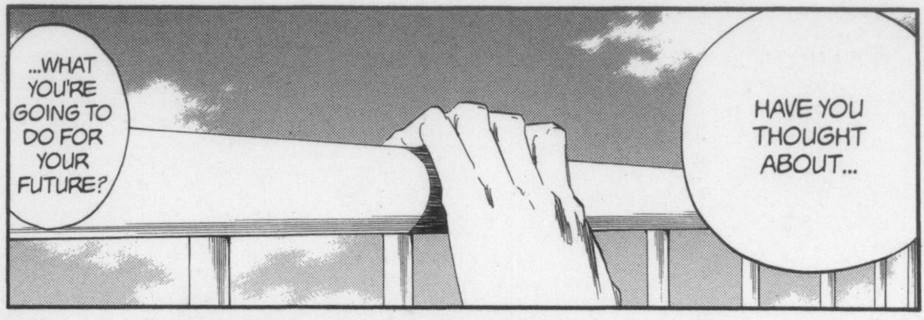
HAVE YOU THOUGHT ABOUT...
...WHAT YOU'RE GOING TO DO FOR YOUR FUTURE?

YOU MEAN LIKE FOR A CAREER OR COLLEGE?

DUH!
WHAT ELSE IS THERE?

I THOUGHT I STILL HAD TIME.
THE CAREER COUNSELING WILL BE AT THE END OF THE SEMESTER.
YOU GOTTA START THINKING ABOUT IT.
TMP
WHEN YOU FIRST GOT INTO THIS SCHOOL, YOU HAD GOOD GRADES, BUT OVER THE PAST YEAR, THEY'VE DROPPED.
SHUT IT. I HAD A LOT OF THINGS ON MY MIND, SO I COULDN'T HELP LET-TING THEM SLIP.
BESIDES, I'M STILL ABOVE THE AVERAGE.

I WONDER WHAT RUKIA'S UP TO.

WHAT'S RUKIA GOT TO DO WITH ANYTHING?

I'M JUST SAYING, WOULD IT KILL HER TO POP IN AND SAY HELLO FROM TIME TO TIME?

DON'T YOU THINK IT'S COLD OF HER TO NOT SHOW HER FACE EVEN ONCE SINCE THEN?

IT'S NOT COLD.

SHE'S NOT IN CHARGE OF KARAKURA TOWN ANY MORE, SO IT'S COMPLETELY NORMAL FOR HER TO NOT HANG AROUND.

YOU DON'T MISS HER?

NO REASON TO.

READ THIS WAY

I FINALLY HAVE A NORMAL LIFE AFTER SIXTEEN YEARS.
I'D BE FINE WITH THIS PEACE AND QUIET UNTIL THE DAY I DIE.

YOU GOT A POINT THERE.
I DON'T WANT TO GO THROUGH THAT TRAUMATIC STUFF AGAIN.

THAT'S RIGHT.

I NEVER FELT SUPERIOR FOR BEING ABLE TO SEE GHOSTS.
I NEVER THOUGHT I COULD MAKE A LIVING...
...OR SAVE SOMEBODY'S LIFE WITH IT.
ALL IT MADE ME DO ...
...WAS CRAVE A LIFE WHERE I DIDN'T HAVE TO SEE THEM.
AND NOW I'VE GOT WHAT I'VE ALWAYS WANTED.

HEY!
HEY, YOU!

BUMP
OW!
HOLD IT RIGHT THERE!
GIVE ME BACK MY BAG!!
MIZUIRO.

ACTUALLY...

READ
THIS
WAY

HOLD THIS FOR ME.
FWUMP

...TO PROVE I WAS A SOUL REAPER.

THERE'S ONE MORE THING I STILL HAVE...

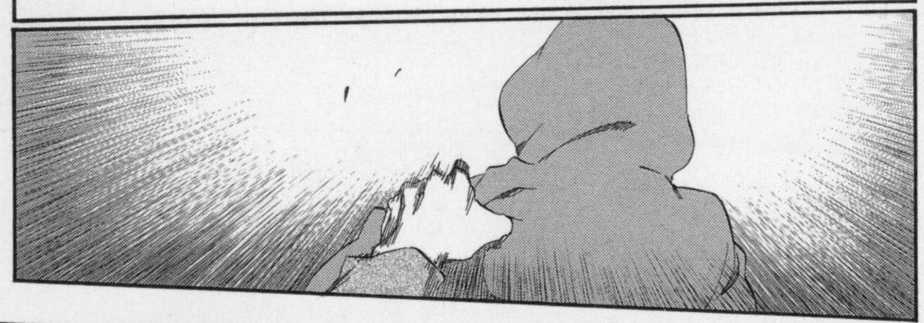

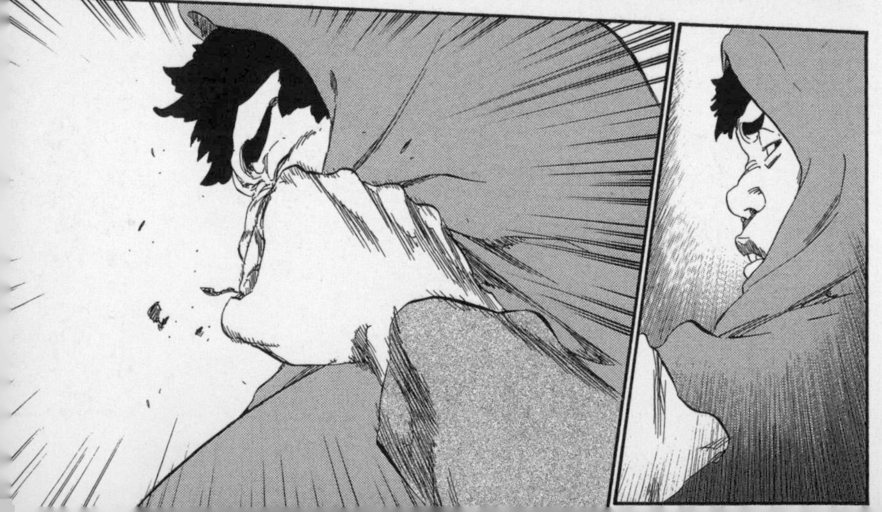

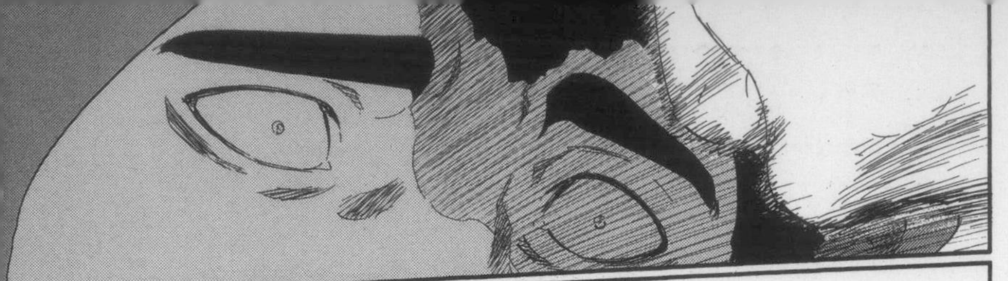

THE BODY AND REFLEXES I FORGED TO WIN THE BATTLE...

...COME IN HANDY NOW AND THEN.

WOOOOOW!!
WHAT WAS THAT? I'M IMPRESS-ED, KID!
THANKS!

YOU MUST BE HUNGRY! LET ME TREAT YOU TO A BOWL OF RAMEN.
YOU IN?
NO THANKS.

I WOULDN'T WANNA GET IN TROUBLE LATER.
PLEASE KEEP THE FACT THAT I PUNCHED THAT GUY A SECRET.

HUH?
OKAY...
THAT'S TOO BAD.

WHAT DO YOU KNOW ...

YOU'RE MORE CAUTIOUS THAN I THOUGHT.

BLEACH424.

The Lost Agent

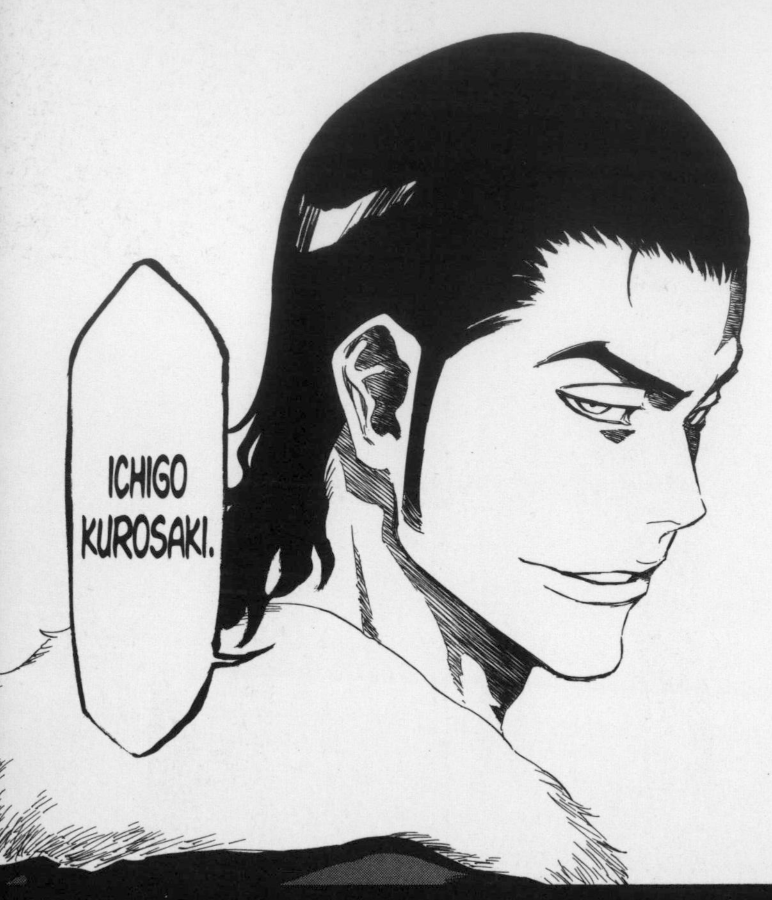
ICHIGO KUROSAKI.

THE LOST AGENT ARC

WHAT'S THE DEAL WITH ME NOT HAVING A GIRLFRIEND YET?
WHAT MAKES YOU THINK YOU WOULD EVER HAVE ONE?

HOW LONG YOU GONNA SLEEP FOR, ICHIGO?
I'LL WAKE YOU UP WITH MY FIST!

YOU WON'T AWAKEN?
ICHIGO KUROSAKI.

425. A Day Without Melodies

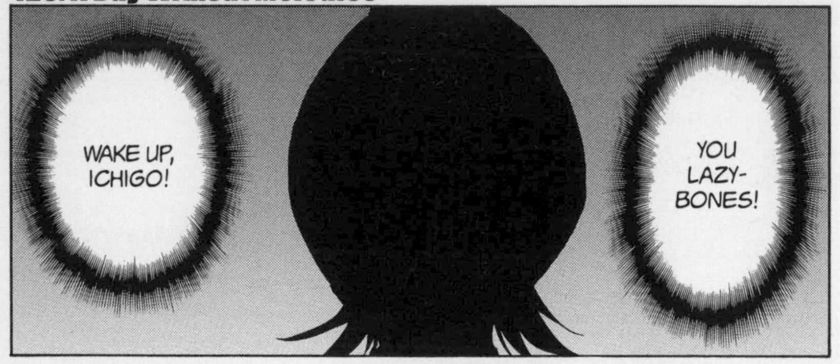
YOU LAZY-BONES!
WAKE UP, ICHIGO!

WAKE UUUUP !!
THUD THUD THUD
THUD THUD
I...
...CHI...

...GOO...

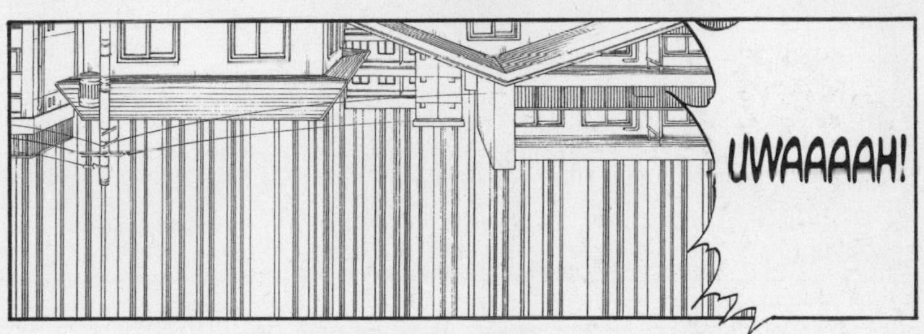
UWAAAAH!

Y...
YOU IDIOT! ARE YOU CRAZY ?!
WHAT IF I'D FALLEN ?!
WHAT IF I'D DIED ?!
I DUNNO.
WHEN YOU DIE, YOU GO TO THE SOUL SOCIETY, I GUESS.
WELL, WELL...
LOOK WHO HAS THE CLEVER MOUTH!

READ THIS WAY

AND ANYWAY, A TWO-STORY FALL ISN'T ABOUT TO KILL YOU.
THANKS TO YOU I HAD THIS WEIRD DREAM. YOU CAN MAKE UP FOR IT BY FALLING NOW.
STRAAAAAIN
WAAAH! AAAAH! DON'T DO IT, I'LL FALL! I REALLY WILL!!

...?
STRANGE DREAM?
WHAT ABOUT?

WHAT WAS IT...?

I CAN'T REMEMBER NOW THAT I MENTIONED IT.

425
A Day Without Melodies
BLEACH

SO.
HOW MUCH WILL IT BE?

FIVE...
5,000 YEN...

WHAT? 5,000 YEN FOR A WEEK?! DON'T WASTE MY TIME! NEXT!!
YANK
AAW!
SIR, YES, SIR!
I AM SATODA, VICE-CAPTAIN OF THE SOCCER CLUB! WE WISH TO BORROW YOUR TALENT, MR. KUROSAKI!
YEAH, YEAH. STATE YOUR TERMS AND PRICE.
ICHI-GO...
HM?

HE'S BARGAINING RIGHT NOW.
THIS'LL TAKE A WHILE.
AH.
I SEE.
I FORGOT HIS LEASE WITH THE BASKETBALL TEAM IS UP.
THIS SUCKS. NOW ICHIGO WON'T BE ABLE TO HANG OUT WITH ME AGAIN.
YOU MAKE IT SOUND LIKE YOU GUYS USUALLY DO.

W...
WE DO!!
IT'S NOT LIKE I'VE GOT A LOT OF TIME ON MY HANDS AND HANG AROUND THE PLACE HE WORKS TO INVITE HIM OUT UNTIL HE GETS SICK OF ME!!
SURE, SURE.

I DON'T REMEMBER ICHIGO BEING THE TYPE TO BE SO CONCERNED ABOUT MONEY.
WE NEED SOMEONE TO PLAY KEEPER!
IF IT'S A GOALKEEPER YOU NEED, WHY NOT GO WITH CHAD?
HE'S PROBABLY SAVING UP FOR HIS POST-GRADUATION PLANS.
TO GET A PLACE OF HIS OWN AND STUFF.
SADO DECIDED TO GO FOR A PART-TIME JOB THAT PAYS BETTER THAN US!
HUH ?!
HE'S MOVING OUT?!
WELL, I DON'T KNOW THAT FOR SURE.

READ THIS WAY

EITHER WAY, ICHIGO'S DAD DOESN'T SEEM THE TYPE TO LEND HIM MONEY FOR WHATEVER HE MIGHT DECIDE TO DO.
I THINK IT'S A GOOD IDEA FOR HIM TO SAVE AS MUCH AS HE CAN NOW.

AH...
WHEN YOU PUT IT THAT WAY—
THANK YOU SO VERY MUCH!

CHEEEEER
YOU DID IT!
NICE! LET'S GO TELL THE CAPTAIN!

YOU DECIDED TO GO WITH THE SOCCER CLUB?
FOR HOW MUCH?

I'M NOT TELL-ING.

START-ING WHEN?

TODAY!

HEEY
ONE TWO ONE

WHAT THE?!

WHAT HAPPENED TO BASKET-BALL?
AH! IT'S ARISAWA!

MY CONTRACT WITH THEM ENDED LAST WEEK.
WHAT ABOUT YOUR CLUB RESPON-SIBILITIES?
I'VE GOT WORK.
DIDN'T I TELL YOU? LAST MONTH I STARTED TEACHING AT OUR DOJO.

YOU? AN INSTRUCTOR?
GOOD THING I QUIT WHEN I DID. NO WAY WOULD I EVER WANNA CALL YOU MASTER.
I COULD MAKE YOU CALL ME THAT NOW IF I WANTED TO.
HMMMM HM HM HMMM HM. ♪

HMMMM HM HM HM HM HM HMMMM. ♪

3-1
THERE GOES ORIHIME.
SHE'S REALLY SOMETHING ELSE. LIKE AN IDOL.
THE MOMENT I LAID EYES ON HER, I KNEW I'D MADE THE RIGHT DECISION TO COME TO THIS SCHOOL.
I GOT A GREAT SHOT OF HER WITH MY CELL PHONE THE OTHER DAY.
SERIOUS?! SEND IT TO ME!

HM?
YOO-HOO!

ICHIGO!!
TATSUKI!!
OH, IT'S INOUE...
HEE-YAH!
LUNGE
SLIIIIIIDE
YOU IDIOT, THAT'S DANGEROUS! YOU COULD FALL!!
WE CAN TOTALLY SEE YOUR PANTIES!

OUCH!

OF COURSE! NEXT TIME YOU DO SOMETHING SO DANGEROUS, I'LL PUMMEL YOU EVEN HARDER!
EVEN HARDER THAN THIS?!
YOU'LL BREAK MY HEAD!
NO NEED TO FLIP OUT ON HER.
IT'S NOT LIKE SHE GOT HURT.

QUIET! YOU'VE GOT NO RIGHT TO GRIPE ABOUT HOW I DISCIPLINE ORIHIME!
I'M NOT GRIPING! I'M JUST SAYING GIVE HER A BREAK!
THAT'S CALLED GRIPING!
UM... HEY!
I ACTUALLY HAVE SOMETHING I WANTED TO ASK YOU TWO!
ASK?
YEAH.
ACTUALLY ...

IT'S ABOUT THE "WAHAHA SONG" THAT I USE FOR THE THEME SONG OF MY LIFE AND I'M TRYING TO FIND THE RIGHT PLACES FOR THE DO RE MI AND...
IN THE RIGHT PLACE WHAT EXACTLY ?
AND LATELY, I'VE ONLY BEEN ABLE TO HUM IT!
THAT'S A GOOD THING, RIGHT?
WHY DO YOU THINK THAT IS?!
BE-CAUSE YOU'VE FINALLY GROWN UP?

WROOOOOOOONG!
WHOA!
HOW'D YOU MAKE YOUR EYES LOOK LIKE 3'S?!
ORI-HIME'S GOTTEN BETTER AT MAKING FACES.
THE COR-RECT AN-SWER IS!
IT'S BECAUSE I COULDN'T DE-CIDE WHETHER TO PLACE THE "DO" WITH "DOKURO-DAN" OR "DOBUROKU"!
DO
CHOCOLATE

DOKURO-DAN MEANS "SKULL CLAN" AND "DOBUROKU" MEANS "UNREFINED SAKE"

WHICH DO YOU THINK WOULD BE BETTER?
WHICHEVER.
AH!
I ALMOST FORGOT! I DON'T HAVE TIME FOR THIS!

WHAT IS IT, TATSUKI?
WORK!
YOU'VE GOT IT TOO, RIGHT, ORIHIME? YOU BETTER GET HOME.
SOUNDS TOUGH. GOOD LUCK.
YOU ACT LIKE THIS HAS NOTHING TO DO WITH YOU, BUT YOU CALLED YOUR JOB, RIGHT?

YOUR BOSS CHEWED YOU OUT LAST TIME!
DON'T BLAME ME FOR WHAT HAPPENS IF YOU DON'T CALL IN.
KURO-SAKI!!
COME JOIN PRAC-TICE NOW!

KUROSAKI—
TOSS
HUH?

YOU IDIOT!!

DO YOU HEAR YOURSELF ?!
FIRST, YOU TAKE LAST WEEK OFF, THEN YOU ONLY COME IN ONE DAY, AND NOW YOU'RE ASKING TO TAKE ANOTHER WEEK OFF?!
I KNOW, AND I SAID I'M SORRY...
SORRY DOESN'T CUT IT! YOU'VE GOT A LOTTA NERVE, YOU KNOW THAT?!

GET YOUR BUTT DOWN HERE, OR YOU'RE FIRED!
AW, REALLY ?
WELL, THEN I GUESS THERE'S NOTHING I CAN DO.
WHAT ?!
NO, NO! LISTEN, DON'T TALK LIKE THAT, ICHIGO...
I REALLY AM SORRY.
AND I APPRECIATE ALL THE TIME I'VE WORKED FOR YOU.
I'M JUST SAYING IF YOU HAVE TO FIRE ME FOR BEING A SLACKER WHO WANTS TO TAKE TIME OFF, IT CAN'T BE HELPED.
IT HASN'T BEEN THAT MUCH TIME! ONLY SIX MONTHS! YOU HAVE YET TO SEE THE FUN THAT WORKING ODD JOBS OFFERS!

THIS IS ONLY THE BEGINNING OF A GRAND ADVENTURE TOGETHER—
CLICK
THANK YOU FOR READING.
BEEP
MMMMMMK!!

BADUM

WE'RE LOOKING FOR...
...THE ONE NAMED KUROSAKI!

MURMUR MURMUR
SHOW YOURSELF!

WHAT ERA ARE THOSE GOONS FROM?
I DON'T KNOW ANYBODY SO OLD-SCHOOL.

ONE OF OUR BOYS LOST SEVEN TEETH THANKS TO HIM!
SEVEN!!
WHEN TWO IS MORE THAN ENOUGH!
A-HAAA.
I SEE NOW.

HEH HEH HEH. I'M SURE YOU HEAR ME, KUROSAKI! YOU'RE PROBABLY SHAKING IN YOUR BOOTS WONDERING HOW I LEARNED YOUR NAME!
IT WAS EASY! WE GOT A GOOD LOOK AT YOUR FACE! IT WAS A PIECE OF CAKE PUTTING TWO AND TWO TOGETHER!

BA-BOOM
BUT LISTEN UP, KURO-SAKI! UNTIL YOU COME OUT...
...WE OF THE MIYA HIGH GANG ARE BLOCKADING THIS GATE!
YOU THERE!
DROP THE RETRO DISPLAY.
CAN'T YOU SEE YOU'RE IN-CONVEN-IENCING EVERY-ONE?
ZSH

NOW THEN.
FOR BEING KUROSAKI'S FRIENDS, YOU SEEM PRETTY CLEVER.
I'M SURE YOU CAN UNDER-STAND WHAT I'M TELLING YOU.
ZSH
ZSH
ZSH
SO.
HURRY ALONG HOME.

OH YEAH ?!
AND JUST WHO ARE YOU?!
ARE YOU KUROSAKI ?!

WHAT DID YOU SAY?

WH-WHAT DID YOU DO?!

WHUDDDD

NOT TAKING US SERIOUSLY, DUMB-ASS?!

THAT'S MY LINE.

I THOUGHT YOU SAID YOU GOT A GOOD LOOK AT HIS FACE.

SO WHAT PART OF ME LOOKS LIKE KUROSAKI?

WHO'S THIS FOUR-EYES THINK HE IS?!

I TAKE BACK WHAT I SAID.

YOU DON'T HAVE TO GO ANYWHERE.

IN FACT...

I DON'T THINK A SINGLE ONE OF YOU WILL BE ABLE TO LEAVE WHEN I'M THROUGH WITH YOU.

THAT BLOCK-HEAD!
DASH
DID HE COME JUST TO STIR THINGS UP?!

WAAAAH!
SKFF

I THINK WHAT EVERYONE'S WONDERING MOST ABOUT WITH THIS NEW ARC...
...IS HOW MY HAIR'S CHANGED.
YEAH, I DON'T THINK SO.

THUD THUD THUD
YOU'RE...
...DEAD...
THUD THUD THUD THUD THUD
MEEEEEEAT!!
GRAB

426. The Starter 2

OOF!!

AND ONE!
TWO!
OW OW OW OW OW OW OW OW !!
WHAT THE?! WHO ARE YOU?! I GIVE UP!!

WH...
WHO THE HELL ARE YOU?!

IT'S...
IT'S H-H-H-H-HIM, MR. OBUTA!
HE'S THE ONE ?!

ELEVEN!
TWELVE!
I GIVE IN! I GIVE IN!!
STOP OR YOU'LL BREAK MY LEG!!

THIR-TEE—
OOF!

WHAT'D YOU DO THAT FOR, ISHIDA?!
THAT'S WHAT I SHOULD BE ASKING YOU.
WHAT'RE YOU DOING HERE, KUROSAKI?
WHAT DO YOU THINK! I SHOWED UP TO TAKE YOUR PLACE!

I SEE NOW.
THAT ORANGE HAIR IS JUST AS I HEARD.
SO YOU'RE ...
...KURO-SAKI!!

Bleach 426. The Starter 2

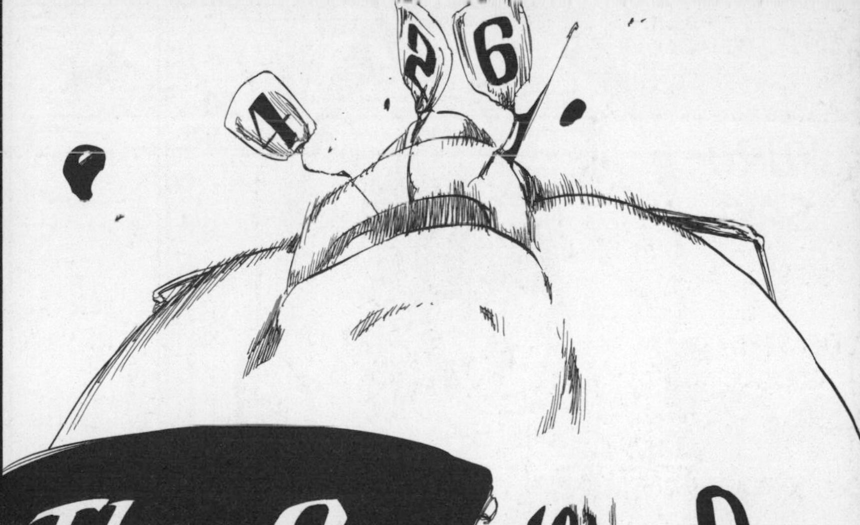

THESE GUYS CAME LOOKING FOR ME! IF THIS IS NONE OF YOUR BUSINESS, THEN GET LOST!
RAWR
WELL I JUST MADE IT MY BUSI-NESS! SO YOU BACK OFF!
SKFF
WHEN YOU COME AROUND, THINGS JUST GET WORSE! REMEMBER THAT YOU'RE SUPPOSED TO BE THE CLASS PRESIDENT! YOU IDIOT!
WHAT?!

QUIT FIGHTING WITH HIM!
YOU'RE SUPPOSED TO BE FIGHTING US, KUROSAKI!!

AND ANOTHER THING!!

BASH

YOU'VE BEEN GOING ON TOO MANY HOLLOW HUNTS LATELY!
THEY'RE NOT HOLLOW HUNTS! THEY'RE HOLLOW EXTERMI-NATIONS!
IF THE SOUL SOCIETY NOTICES, THEN WHAT?!
DON'T SAY IT LIKE I'M DOING IT FOR THE THRILL OR SOME-THING!
AND I'VE ONLY BEEN GOING WHEN THE URAHARA SHOP SENDS A REQUEST!

READ THIS WAY

URAHARA SHOULD BE KEEPING THINGS IN CHECK AS FAR AS THAT GOES.
SO THERE SHOULDN'T BE A PROBLEM!
BASH
DID YOU FORGET THAT UNTIL RECENTLY HE WAS WANTED BY THE SOUL SOCIETY?

BAM

WE SHOULDN'T EVEN BE TALKING ABOUT THAT STUFF RIGHT NOW! EMAIL ME ABOUT IT LATER!
FLIP
I DON'T KNOW YOUR EMAIL ADDRESS!
AND SINCE WHEN DO YOU HAVE A PHONE?!
MR. URAHARA GAVE ME ONE FOR HELPING OUT AT THE SHOP THE OTHER DAY!
THAT PHONE PROBABLY DOESN'T WORK HERE THEN.

KUROSAKIIII!!

BADOOM
YOOOOO, KURO-SAKIII...
IT'S BEEN A LONG TIME.
鬼強

I'M GLAD TO SEE YOU'RE LOOKING WELL.
YOU RECOG-NIZE ME, DON'T YOU?

POOOOOOOOF
YOKOCHIN!

*DEMON STRENGTH

YOKO-CHIN!
YOKOCHIN!
POOOOSH
I TOLD YOU NOT TO CALL ME THAT!

NOPE, DON'T REMEM-BER.
DON'T GIVE UP!!

YOU WERE FLASHING BACK JUST NOW, WEREN'T YOU! SO DON'T GIVE UP!
TRY TO REMEMBER!
I DON'T CARE. I DON'T REMEMBER YOU IN THE FIRST PLACE, AND YOU CHANGING YOUR HAIRDO A LITTLE DOESN'T HELP EITHER.
WHY SHOULD I REMEMBER YOU ANYWAY? THE NERVE!
VERY FUNNY.
I DON'T WANNA HEAR YOUR LIFE STORY.
IMMEDIATELY AFTER YOU BEAT ME UP, I HAD TO MOVE FOR MY DAD'S JOB. I FINALLY COME HOME AFTER FOUR YEARS AND THIS IS WHAT I GET.

I'LL KILL ...
YOU— OOF!
STOMP!

YOKO-CHIN!
BFFF!
SKIDDDDD
YOU OKAY, YOKO-CHIN?!
EE...
LOOM
W-WHO ARE YOU?!
THWACK
BASH
CRACK
THUD
CRUNCH

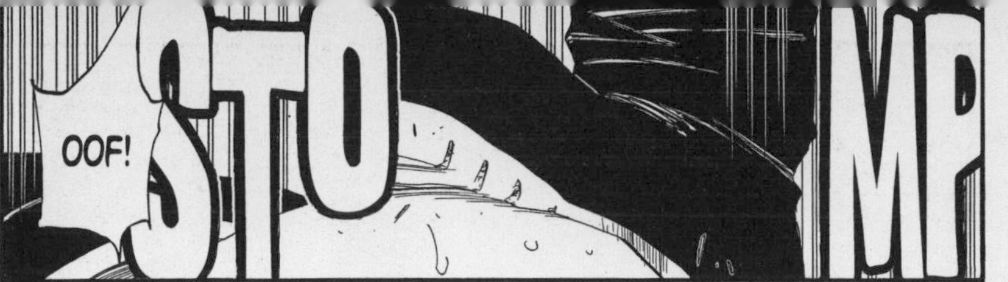

YOU LOOK LIKE YOU'RE HAVING FUN.

ICHIGO.

KURO-SAKI.
SHE'S TALKING TO YOU.
WHO IS SHE?

MY BOSS!
WHAT?!
YOU'RE ALWAYS SKIPPING WORK WITH SOME CLEVER EXCUSE.
BUT YOU'RE NOT GETTING OFF THE HOOK THAT EASILY.

BE A GOOD LITTLE BOY...

...AND BE ABDUCTED BY ME!

NO THANKS!

STRAAAIN
OW OW OW!
LEGGO—
SHOVE
THUD
SHUT
SLAM

VROOOOOOOM
WOW.
SHE WAS ABLE TO TIE KUROSAKI UP AND TAKE HIM AWAY IN A SECOND.
WHAT KIND OF WOMAN IS SHE?
TEACHER!
ICHIGO'S BEEN KID-NAPPED!
WHAT ?!

WHUMP
OW!

UNAGIYA
CHEAP! FAST! SAFE!
FROM CAT-SITTING TO PERSON-TRACKING, WE DO IT ALL!

THIS HURTS! GET THIS TAPE OFF ME!
ONLY IF YOU PROMISE NOT TO RUN AWAY.
PAT PAT
THAT'S JUST WHAT A KIDNAPPER WOULD SAY!
BRRRING
THE PHONE'S RINGING!

HELLO AND WHAT CAN I DO FOR YOU?
KLATCH
WE'RE CHEAP! FAST! AND SAFE! WE'RE THE UNAGIYA!
HUH?!

YOU WANT TWO SPECIALS?! YOU FOOL, WE'RE NOT AN EEL SHOP!!
HUH?!
SURE, WE'RE CALLED UNAGIYA!
BUT THAT'S JUST THE NAME OF OUR BUSINESS, BLOCK-HEAD!
UM, I'VE SAID IT BEFORE, BUT YOU REALLY OUGHT TO CHANGE THE NAME OF YOUR BUSINESS.
KLATCH
WHAT?!

*UNAGIYA MEANS "EEL SHOP" BUT ALSO HAPPENS TO BE THE BOSS'S LAST NAME

YOU'RE SUGGESTING I CHANGE MY PRECIOUS NAME THAT'S BEEN PASSED DOWN FOR GENERATIONS?!

NEVER!!

OWNER OF THE ODD JOBS SHOP "UNAGIYA"

IKUMI UNAGIYA

THAT'S NOT WHAT I MEAN.
YOU CAN KEEP YOUR NAME, DUDE, JUST CHANGE THE NAME OF THE SHOP.
NO TO BOTH!
RUMMAGE
AND DON'T CALL ME "DUDE"!
CALL ME MISS IKUMI!
FWAP
HERE'S YOUR WORK!

WE'VE GOT ONE FROM MRS. KONDO IN DISTRICT 2 OF MASHIBA TO WATCH AFTER HER RABBIT!
ONE FROM A MRS. FUKUSHIMA FROM DISTRICT 6 TO COLLECT HER RAT TRAPS!
ANOTHER FROM MR. YAMASHITA FROM DISTRICT 1 OF MINAMIKAWASE TO DO SOME YARD WORK!
AND THERE ARE MORE! ALL THESE ORDERS HAVE BEEN PILING UP WHILE YOU'VE BEEN OUT!

WHAT GIVES! YOU COULD DO THOSE ALL YOURSELF!
I'VE GOT ENOUGH STUFF KEEPING ME BUSY!
WHY DO YOU THINK I HIRED YOU IN THE FIRST PLACE ?!

MOMMMMY!
WHERE ARE YOUUUU?
CRAP!
FWAP
ZSH
FLOP
KLATCH
MOMMY!

I'M HUNGRYYYY.

AAAW, ARE YOU OKAY, MY SWEET LITTLE KAORU? ♡

YOU'VE COME TO THE OFFICE AGAIN WITHOUT YOUR SHOES! NAUGHTY CHILD!
I COULDN'T HELP IT.

OH!
STUPID KUROSAKI'S HERE!
OH, MY.
WHAT'RE YOU DOING HERE?

JUST BECAUSE MY MOM'S A HOTTIE, DON'T GO ACTING ALL FAMILIAR WITH HER!
NYAAAAAAH!
NOW NOW, YOU GO OVER THERE.
I'LL BE RIGHT WITH YOU.
...

SORRY, YOU'RE THE ONLY PERSON HE JUST WON'T TAKE TO.
I KNOW YOU HAVE A LOT YOU WANT TO GET OFF YOUR CHEST, BUT JUST HOLD ON A LITTLE LONGER.
STUFF I WANT TO GET OFF MY CHEST ...
LIKE HOW I'VE GOT ZERO INTEREST IN OLD LADIES?
BONK

THAT HURT! I ONLY SAID THAT CUZ YOU SAID I HAD THINGS TO GET OFF MY CHEST!
I DIDN'T MEAN YOU HAD TO ACTUALLY SAY THEM!
I MEANT FOR YOU TO KEEP THEM TO YOURSELF!
RRRRIP
I'M GONNA TAKE THE TAPE OFF NOW, SO GET TO WORK!!
DING DONG
!
A CLIENT ?
HELLO, PLEASE COME IN.
KLATCH

W...
SNUG
HE'S HUGE.
WELCOME...

!
YOU'RE THAT GUY FROM BEFORE!

SWF

HOW ABOUT...

...SOME RAMEN?

NO NEED.

WE'RE AN EEL SHOP HERE.

NO, WE'RE NOT.

UNAGI

I THINK I'LL USE THESE PAGES...
...TO COVER THE CHANGES IN MY HAIR OVER THOSE BLANK 17 MONTHS.
YOU REALLY THINK ANYONE CARES ABOUT THAT?

URYU!!

ORI-
HIME
?
IS IT TRUE THAT ICHIGO'S BEEN KID-NAPPED ?!

KID-
NAPPED
...
WELL, I'M SURE IT'D LOOK THAT WAY TO THE CASUAL OBSERVER.
BUT...

427. A Delicious Dissonance

WAIT!
ORIHIME! WHER ARE YOU GOING?!
TO SAVE ICHIGO!
WAIT!
HE'S FINE! THE ONE WHO KIDNAPPED HIM WAS THE BOSS AT THE PLACE HE WORKS!

HIS BOSS?
KUROSAKI SAID SO HIMSELF! THERE'S NO MISTAKE!

YOU'RE SURE IT WASN'T SOME WEIRDO?
WELL, SURE SHE SEEMED WEIRD, BUT EVERYONE HE HANGS OUT WITH IS WEIRD TO A DEGREE!

YOU'RE RIGHT!
THAT GOES FOR ME AND YOU TOO.
HUH?!
WELL... YEAH, I GUESS.

...
BUT STILL.
FOR THE PAST FEW DAYS, I'VE BEEN FEELING THIS STRANGE AIR ABOUT ICHIGO.

HAVE YOU SENSED ANYTHING STRANGE, URYU?

NO.
I HAVEN'T FELT ANY-THING.
BESIDES, KUROSAKI'S ALWAYS HAD A STRANGE AIR ABOUT HIM.

OH, IF YOU'RE CARRYING YOUR BAG, THAT MEANS YOU'RE ON YOUR WAY HOME, RIGHT?
ARE YOU OKAY ON TIME?
AH!

YOU'RE RIGHT! MY BOSS IS GONNA KILL ME!
TMP TMP TMP TMP
SEE YOU TOMORROW !!
TMP

SHE'S RIGHT.

EVEN THOUGH HE'S SUPPOSED TO HAVE LOST HIS SPIRITUAL POWERS, THERE'S BEEN SOMETHING CLINGING AROUND KUROSAKI.

AND THAT SOMETHING IS...

...SPIRITUAL PRESSURE.

427
A Delicious Dissonance

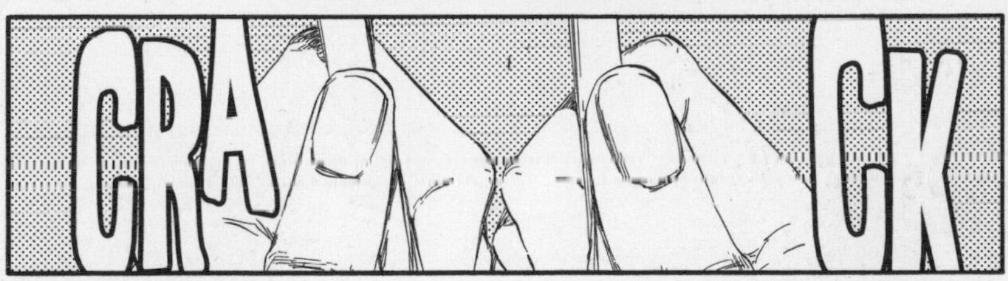
CRA
CK

WELL.
BON APPE- TITE.

HEY.

READ THIS WAY

SIP
I SAID, HEY.

SLUUUURP

I'M TALKIN' TO YOU!
SLAM
WHY ARE YOU EATING RAMEN HERE?!

BECAUSE YOU'RE NOT EATING IT.
EAT IT AT HOME!
AND IF I DON'T EAT IT, IT'LL GO BAD.
WHAT'D YOU COME HERE FOR?!

THIS ISN'T YOUR BREAK AREA!
IT'S MINE!
UNAGI
YOU COME HERE THINKING IT'S YOUR BREAK AREA?

BUT ICHIGO HAS A POINT.
WHAT ARE YOU?
A CLIENT?
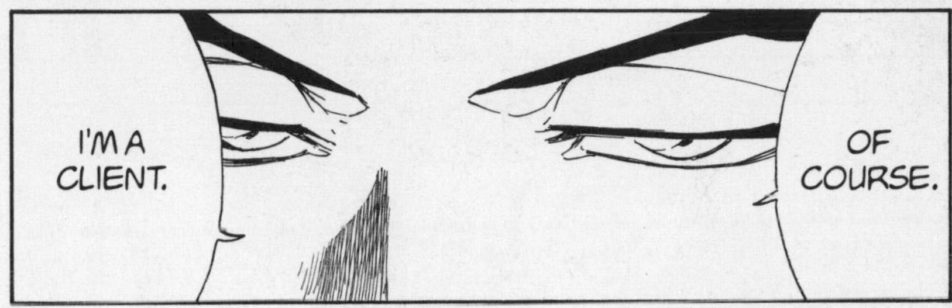
OF COURSE.
I'M A CLIENT.

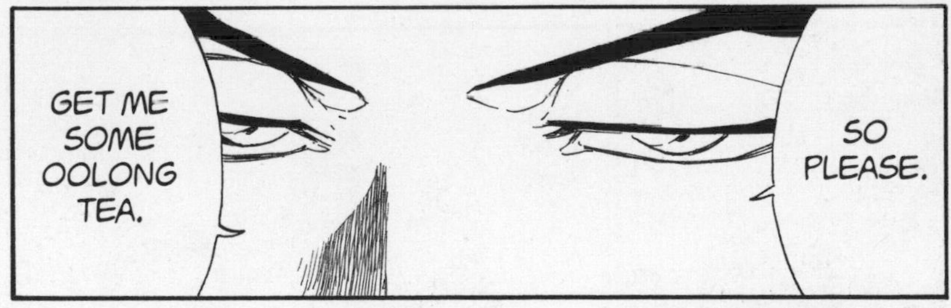
SO PLEASE.
GET ME SOME OOLONG TEA.

IS IT OKAY IF IT'S FROM A BOTTLE?
YOU'RE GONNA SERVE HIM?

GLUG
GLUG
GLUG

SO.
WHAT BUSINESS DO YOU HAVE WITH ME?
THAT'S AWFULLY STRANGE TO SAY.
I'VE GOT NO BUSINESS WITH YOU.

IT WAS PURE CHANCE THAT I CAME TO THIS SHOP.
CONK
I WAS LOOKING FOR A SHOP THAT WOULD TAKE A JOB FOR ME.
CLATTER
AND SAW THE SIGN.
AND WHEN I CAME IN, THERE YOU WERE.
JUST A COINCIDENCE.

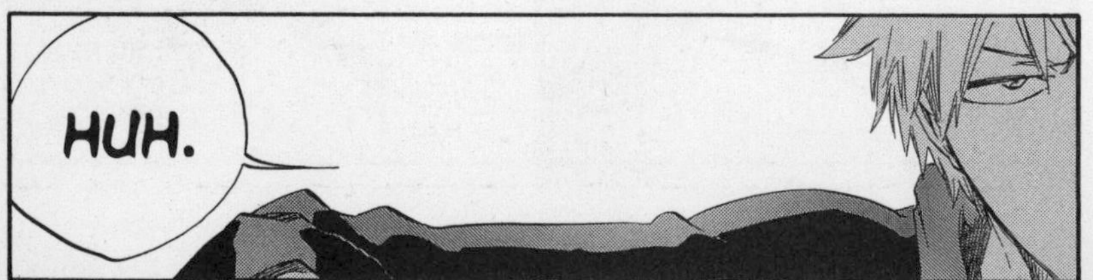
HUH.

IS IT ALSO COINCIDENCE THAT YOU WERE CARRYING AROUND A BOWL OF RAMEN?

AND WHY NOT?
I LIKE RAMEN.
IF YOU'RE GOING TO WALK AROUND WITH SOME-THING BECAUSE YOU LIKE IT...
...THEN I'D BE WALKING AROUND WITH CHOCO-LATE.

YOU LIKE CHOCO-LATE, DO YOU?
HOW ADOR-ABLE.
DON'T TRY TO CHANGE THE SUBJECT.

CLACK

OH, BOY.
I'LL NEVER GET ANYWHERE LIKE THIS.
CLACK

I DIDN'T COME HERE FOR A QUARREL.
YOU, YOUNG LADY. YOU'RE THE OWNER OF THIS SHOP, RIGHT?

YOUNG ...
Y...
YES, THAT'S ME!

IT OKAY...
...IF WE GET DOWN TO BUSINESS?

URAHARA SHOP

WHAP

JINTA HOME-RUN!!

COME TO DADDY!

WHAP
WHIP
OOF!

DON'T GO PLAYING BASEBALL IN FRONT OF OTHER PEOPLE'S HOUSES.
YOU DAMN BRATS.
AND ANOTHER THING...
SCUFF
WHUMP
POP
SNAP
J-JINTA!
THE ONLY ONE WHO CAN PULL OFF A JINTA HOME-RUN...
...IS ME!
BAM

BONK
OOF!

YOU SHOULDN'T THROW A BASEBALL AT SOMEONE WHO'S NOT WEARING A MITT!
FLUMP
I'M SORRY.
IS YOUR BELLY OKAY?

JINTA'S A SILLY BRAT...
...BUT PLEASE PLAY WITH HIM FROM TIME TO TIME.

Y...
YES, URURU!

URAHARA
I'M LOOKING FOR SOMEONE TO DO A PERSONAL BACKGROUND CHECK ON A CERTAIN SOMEBODY.

HIS NAME IS...
ISSHIN KUROSAKI.
HUH?
YOU KNOW THIS MAN?

ARE YOU MOCKING ME?

ISSHIN KUROSAKI'S MY DAD!
IF YOU WANNA KNOW ANYTHING ABOUT HIM, JUST ASK ME!
I'LL ANSWER ANYTHING YOU WANT!

SO HE'S YOUR OLD MAN.
THAT IS A COINCIDENCE.

WHAT DID YOU SAY...?!
BUT...
...WHEN YOU SAY YOU'LL "ANSWER ANYTHING"...

DO YOU REALLY ...

...KNOW ENOUGH ABOUT HIM TO BE ABLE TO ANSWER ANYTHING?

ZSH

IS URAHARA...
...IN?

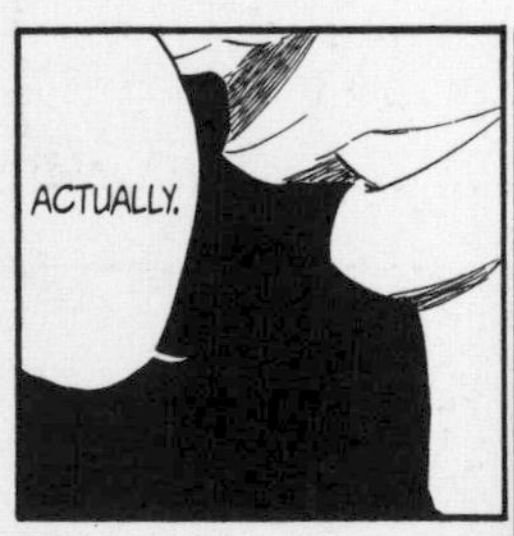
ACTUALLY.

YOU PROBABLY DON'T EVEN KNOW ANYTHING...

...ABOUT YOUR OWN FAMILY.

NOT YET, AT LEAST.

WELL, WELL!
WHAT HAVE WE HERE?

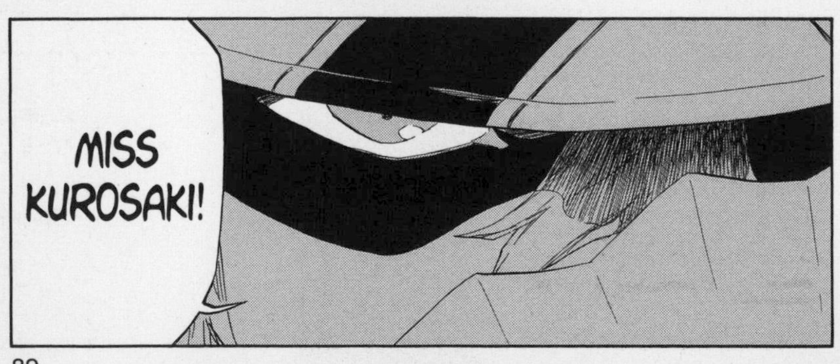
MISS
KUROSAKI!

FIRST IS THE STANDARD HAIRDO.
I HAD THIS UNTIL VOLUME 48.
IT'S ALREADY BEGUN.

BLEACH
ブリーチ

READ THIS WAY

四月
突き出し
WHAT...
...ARE YOU SAYING?

JUST WHAT I SAID.
I'M NOT TRYING TO TALK IN RIDDLES.

HOW MUCH DO YOU REALLY KNOW?
ABOUT YOUR FAMILY...
...I MEAN.
AREN'T THERE SOME THINGS YOU WANT TO LEARN?
LIKE...

WE GOT IT.
JUST LEAVE US THE PHOTO.

SHOP'S CLOSED FOR TODAY.
YOU CAN LEAVE NOW.

WHAT'S ALL THE HURRY ABOUT?
DOES THAT MEAN YOU'LL TAKE THE CASE FOR ME?
WE'LL CALL YOU AFTER WE THINK IT OVER.

I SEE.
FWAP
THEN...
I'LL LEAVE MY NUMBER WITH YOU.
CLACK
KUROSAKI.

GO TO THE URAHARA SHOP YOURSELF.
YOU'LL BE SURE TO SEE SOMETHING VERY INTERESTING THERE.

READ THIS WAY

UNAGIYA
KLATCH
UNA

AAAW.

DID YOU FAIL?

TO GET TURNED DOWN AFTER YOU BROUGHT A GIFT. HOW EM-BARRASS-ING.
THAT'S WHAT HAPPENS WHEN YOU'RE TOO MEAN TO EVEN LET US SEE THIS ICHIGO KID.
PATHETIC.
WHAT ARE YOU DOING HERE?

RIRUKA.
KUTSUZAWA.

I THOUGHT I TOLD YOU NOT TO FOLLOW ME.
OH, DON'T TALK LIKE THAT.
WE'RE COLLEAGUES, THERE'S NO RANK HERE.
WE DON'T HAVE TO LISTEN TO WHAT YOU TELL US.

BUT ANY-WAY, YOU'VE GOT NO PERSUASIVE SKILLS AT ALL!
LET ME DO THIS! I'LL HAVE HIM RIGHT WHERE WE WANT HIM IN NO TIME!
AND YET HE PERSUADED US TO WORK FOR HIM.

SPIN
SHUT UP, GIRIKO!
YOU'RE THE ONLY ONE WHO WAS TALKED INTO THIS! I WASN'T CONVINCED OF ANYTHING AND I DON'T WORK FOR HIM!
TWITCH
ANY-WAY—

KEEP IT DOWN.

THEY'LL HEAR YOU INSIDE.

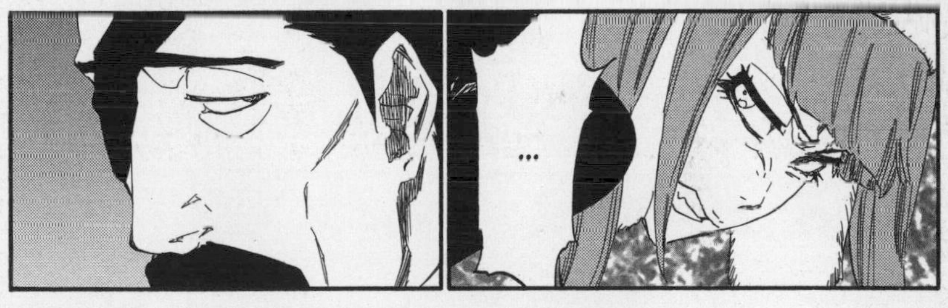

THINGS ARE GOING TO START GETTING GOOD.

URAHARA SHOP

BLEACH

428. The Known

TESSAI, YOU JERK!!

RAWR

SWISH

GRAB

IF YOU KEEP WAILING ON PEOPLE'S HEADS, YOU'LL GIVE 'EM BRAIN DAMAGE!

COME OUT HERE, RIGHT NOW!

GRAB

READ THIS WAY

CRICK CRICK CRICK
CRICK CRICK CRICK
GUUWOOOOOOOOAH!!

GWAH!
BFF HA HA HA HA!!
URURU, CUT IT OUT!!
UHYA HYA!
I'LL KILL YOU, I SWEAR!!
TICKLE TICKLE

SILENCE!
!

RIGHT NOW...
...MISS KARIN IS VISITING THE SHOP.

TA-DA!

← SFX

FOR SHOULDERS AND HIPS THAT HAVE BEEN POSSESSED BY A SPIRIT AND ARE STIFF!

STIFF BE-GONE α

INDOMETHACIN

IT'S THE GHOST MEDICINE RUB, STIFF-BE-GONE ALPHA!!

TA-DA!

OR WHEN YOU DON'T WANT GHOSTS FOLLOWING YOU INTO THE TUB OR TOILET!

SPIRIT REPELLANT SPRAY λ!!

TA-DA!

MAKE A TEMPORARY ESCAPE FROM AN ATTACKING HOLLOW!

IT'S THE ELECTROMAGNETIC CAPTURE BOMB, ZETA BALL!!

ANYTHING ELSE YOU NEED?
NOPE.
HOW ABOUT THIS NEW STIFF-BE-GONE THETA?
TA-DA!
WHAT'S DIFFERENT ABOUT IT?
IT'S GOT VITAMIN C IN IT—
NO THANKS.

ALL RIGHT THEN.
ZIP
YOU'RE SURE I DON'T HAVE TO PAY TODAY EITHER?
PLEASE DON'T MAKE ME SAY IT AGAIN.
YOU'RE FINE.
YOUR BROTHER'S DONE SO MUCH FOR US. ♪

I SEE.

BY THE WAY.
IS HE STILL THE SAME AS EVER?
YEP.
AND YOUR FEELINGS TOO?

YEAH.

IT'S OKAY...
HE DOESN'T NEED TO GET HIS SOUL REAPER POWERS BACK.
MY BROTHER'S ALWAYS FOUGHT.
EVEN BEFORE HE BECAME A SOUL REAPER.

HE HAD TO PROTECT US.
THAT'S WHY HE SAID HE HAD TO FIGHT.
HE'S ALWAYS CARRIED A BURDEN ON HIS SHOULDERS.
SO...
...HE'S FINE THE WAY HE IS NOW.

NOW IT'S OUR TURN...
...TO PROTECT OUR BIG BROTHER.

I'M GOING NOW.

UM.

IF ANY-THING HAP-PENS...
...PLEASE COME TO ME.
I'LL MAKE...
...WHATEVER PREPARATIONS NECESSARY.

I'M JUST SAYING *IF*.

THANKS.

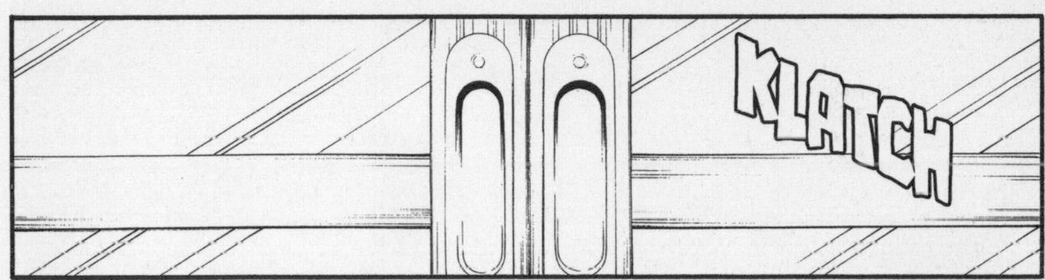
KLATCH

TMP

KARIN ...?
WHAT'S SHE DOING AT URAHARA'S PLACE?

WORRIED?
I DON'T BLAME YOU.
WHEN YOUR OWN LITTLE SISTER'S PAYING VISITS TO SOME SUSPICIOUS GUY'S PLACE.

HE'S NOT SUSPICIOUS.

URAHARA IS—

HE SAVED ...

...US?

HOW MUCH DO YOU KNOW...
...TO THINK THAT YOU KNOW ANYTHING ABOUT THAT URAHARA GUY?

I'M WARNING YOU.
STRIKE WHILE YOU STILL CAN.
IF YOU WANT TO PROTECT YOUR FAMILY.

TELL ME...
...YOUR NAME.

WHAT'S YOUR NAME?
GINJO.

KUGO GINJO.

AFTER LOSING A CHRISTMAS PARTY BET...
...I HAD TO SHAVE MY HEAD INTO A MOHAWK.
THAT MUST'VE BEEN ONE TOUGH CHRISTMAS PARTY BET.
THOUGH IT WAS ME THAT MADE YOU DO IT.

BLEACH

BLEACH
ブリーチ

READ THIS WAY

DON'T GET THE WRONG IDEA.

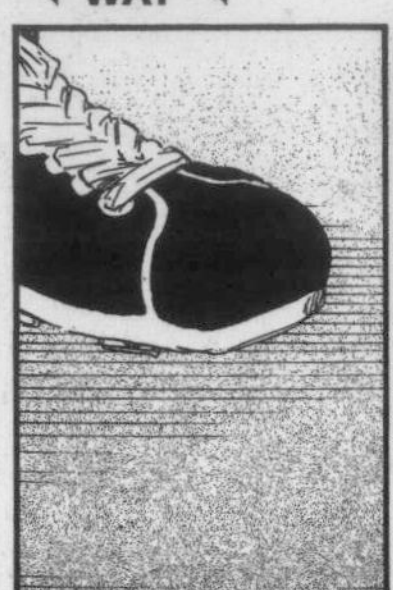

IT'S NOT LIKE I...
...TRUST YOU YET.

I'M SURE.

WELL THEN.

I'LL GIVE YOU THIS.

BLEACH 429.

CLINIC

READ THIS WAY

Welcome to our EXECUTION

WELCOME BACK!

BRO-THER!

BA
95
AM

IT'S OUR FIRST TEST FOR THE SCHOOL YEAR.
AND I GOT A 95!
PRAISE ME!
PRAISE ME!
PRAISE ME!
ISN'T THAT GREAT ?!

GRAB
THAT'S AWESOME, YUZU! GOOD JOB!!
BOOMF
YOU GOTTA SHOW THAT TO DAD! HE'LL BE THRILLED!

SPEAKING OF DAD, WHERE IS HE?
...

I DUNNO.
HE'S BEEN OUT SINCE THIS MORNING.
I SEE.

WELL.

I'LL BE IN MY ROOM.

OH...

BROTHER?

HM?
WHAT IS IT, YUZU?

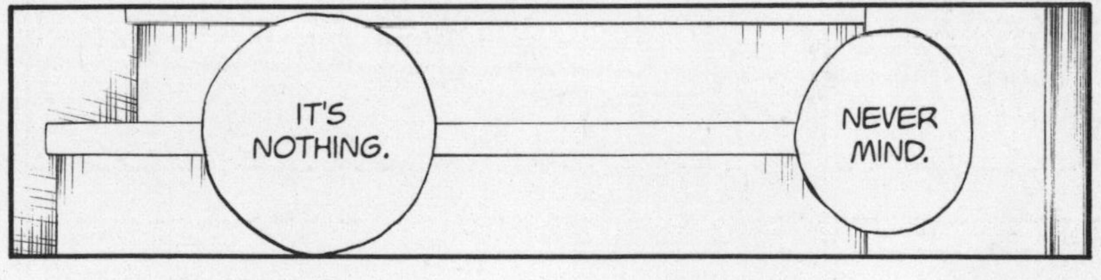
NEVER MIND.
IT'S NOTHING.

THUD

READ
THIS
WAY

WHERE DID THAT BASTARD GO?

IF I HAD MY SOUL REAPER POWERS NOW, I'D BE ABLE TO SENSE HIS SPIRITUAL PRESSURE...

WHAT AM I THINKING?
I GUESS I'M STILL NOT OVER IT.

ICHIIIIIGO!! ICHIIIIIGO!

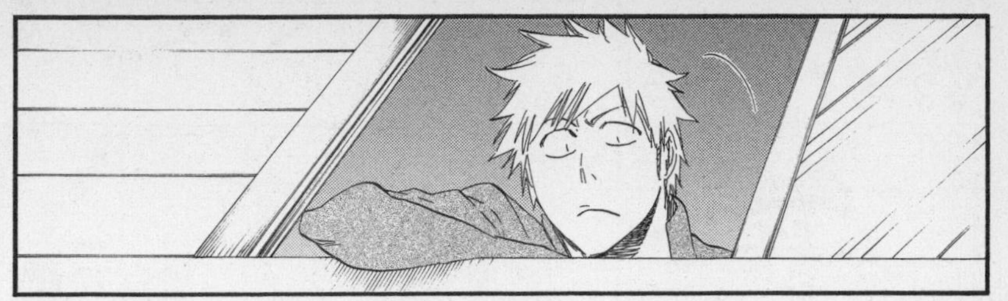

WANT SOME BREAD?!

IT'S A STEAL!

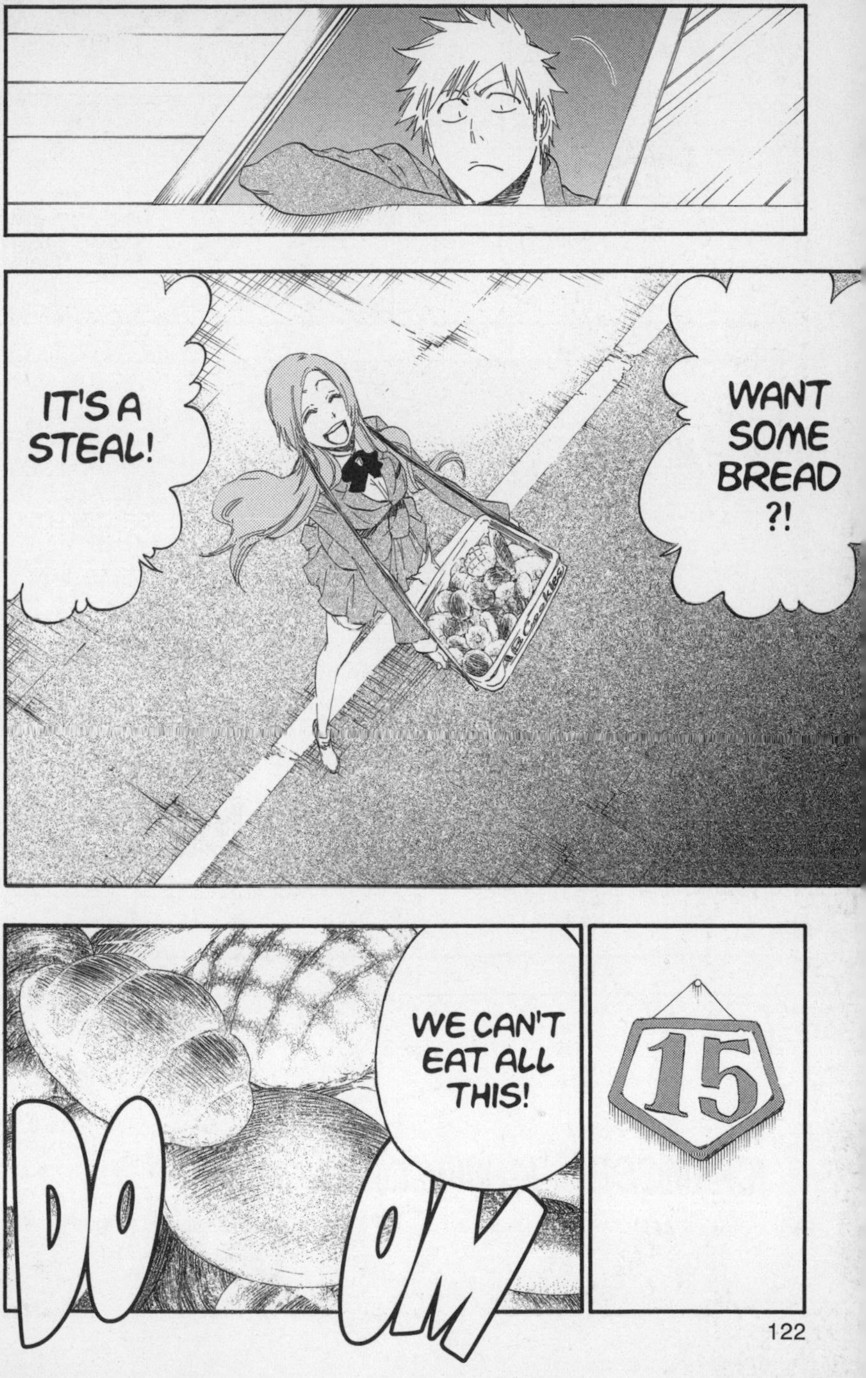

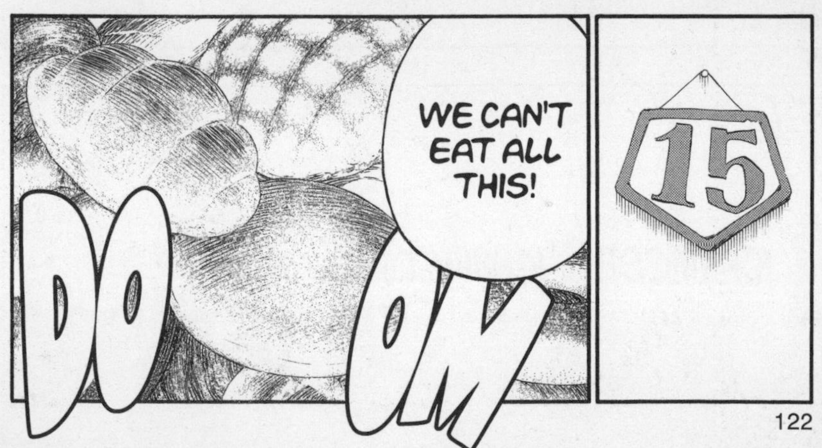
15
WE CAN'T EAT ALL THIS!
DOOM

OH.
REALLY?

REALLY!
WE'RE A FAMILY OF FOUR!
KLAK

I MEAN, WE'LL TAKE WHAT WE CAN, BUT...
WHAT'RE YOU FIDGETING FOR?
FIDGET FIDGET
ROCK ROCK
NO-THING.
I JUST DIDN'T EXPECT TO BE INVITED UPSTAIRS.

IT'S NOT LIKE THIS IS YOUR FIRST TIME IN HERE.
TAKE SOME OF THIS BREAD HOME WITH YOU.
THIS IS JUST THE REJECT BREAD YOUR BOSS GAVE YOU, ISN'T IT?
IT'S NOT THE REJECTS! IT'S THE LEFT-OVERS!
SAME THING.
WELL THE FEELINGS AREN'T!
HEY...

ICHIGO...
HAS SOMETHING HAPPENED RECENTLY?

TWITCH

NO.
WHY DO YOU ASK?

YEAH. IT'S JUST...
I THOUGHT MAYBE YOU WERE BEING FOLLOWED BY SOME STRANGER ...
OR YOU WERE IN TROUBLE OR SOME-THING.
HUH?!
UUUH, A FEELING... I GUESS?
FEEL-ING?

ME?
BEING FOLLOW-ED?
PEOPLE WANNA START STUFF WITH ME ALL THE TIME, BUT FOLLOWED?
YOU'RE A LOT MORE LIKELY TO BE STALKED THAN ME.

I...
I'M NOT THOUGH!
OKAY THEN.
I GUESS MY FEELING WAS OFF THE MARK!

I'M SORRY...
I SHOULDN'T HAVE MADE ASSUMP-TIONS AND GOTTEN WORRIED.
IT'S NO BIG DEAL.
IT'S A GOOD THING THAT YOU DO THAT.
OH, YEAH.
I'LL GIVE YOU BACK THAT COMIC YOU LET ME BORROW.
OH!
IT'S OKAY, I'M IN NO HURRY FOR IT!

!
ZSH

KU
IS THIS SPIRITUAL ENERGY ORIHIME'S?

I GUESS SHE GOT TO HIM FIRST.
I JUST HOPE YOU CAN GET TO THE BOTTOM OF THAT STRANGE FEELING YOU HAD.

WHEN IT COMES TO KUROSAKI, RATHER THAN ASK HIM UP FRONT, IT MIGHT BE EASIER TO GET HIM TO SPILL THE BEANS BY TAKING THE LONG WAY AROUND.
IN CASE ORIHIME CAN'T GET TO THE BOTTOM OF IT, I'LL CHECK AROUND TOWN FOR ANYTHING UNUSUAL FIRST.

WHO'S THAT ?!

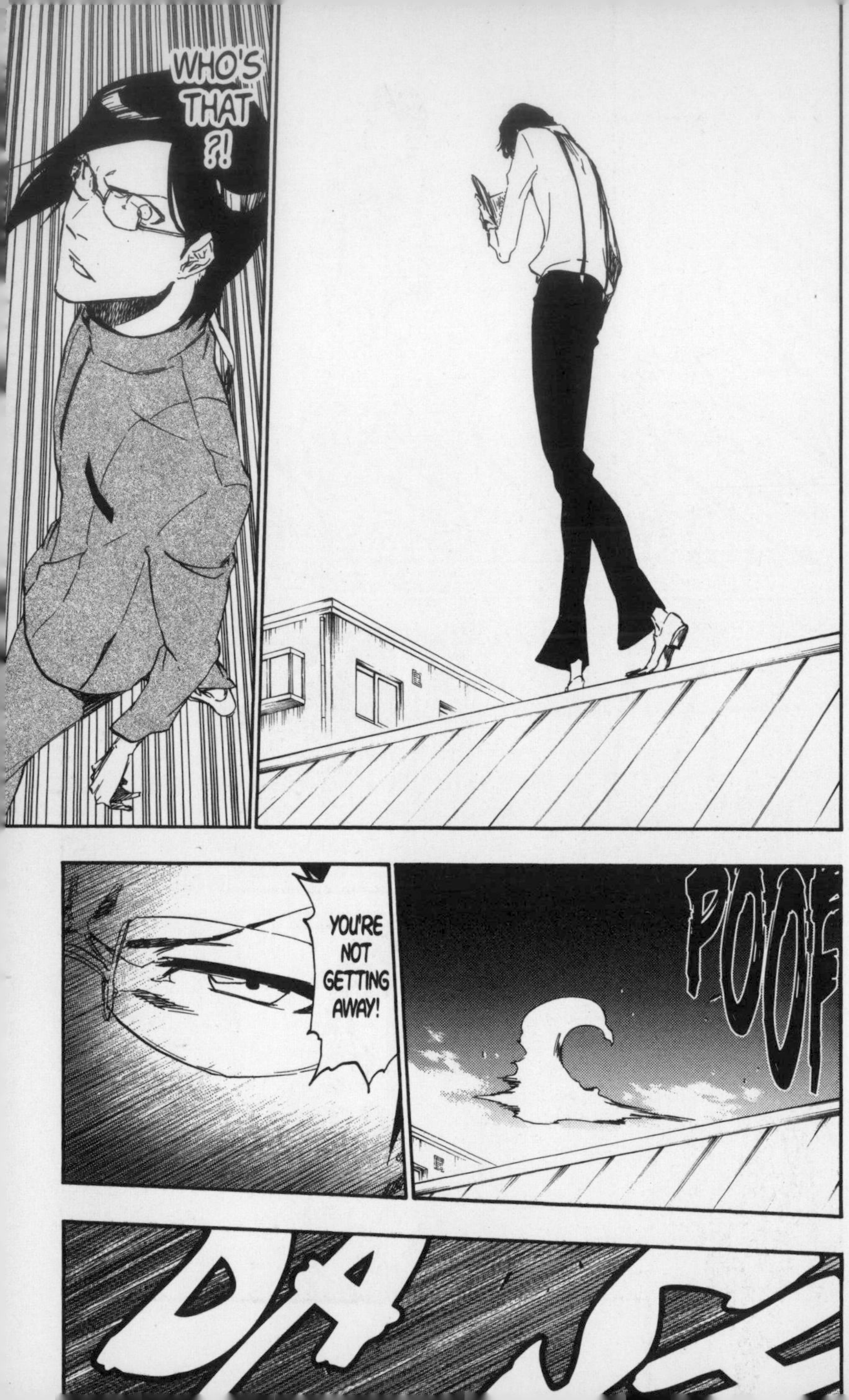

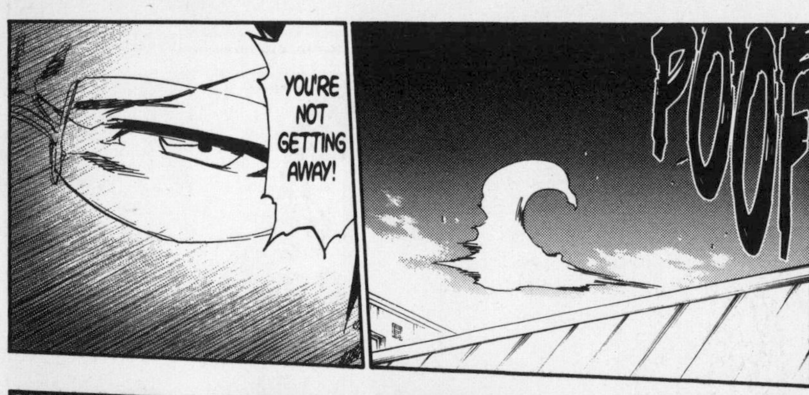
POOF
YOU'RE NOT GETTING AWAY!

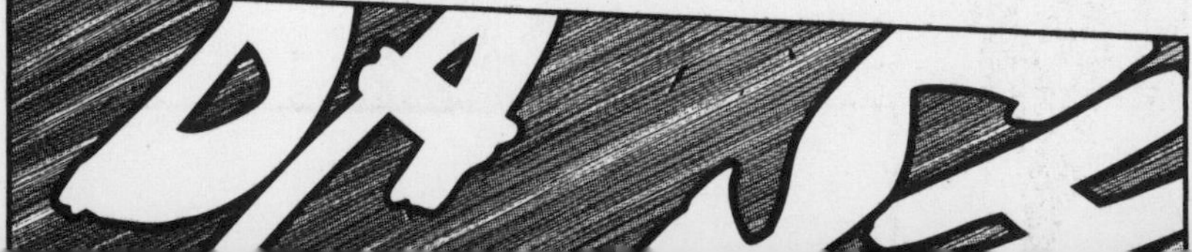
DA

HE'S FAST!
THIS ISN'T HUMAN SPEED!
BUT I CAN'T SEE ANY SPIRITUAL PARTICLE FLUCTUA TIONS AROUND HIM.
WHAT ON EARTH IS ENABLING HIM TO ACCELER- ATE LIKE THAT?!

THMP
HOP
BZZT
BZZT

WHAT WAS THAT LIGHT JUST NOW?

DAMN!

DAD'S...
...STILL NOT BACK YET.

WELL THEN. I'LL GIVE YOU THIS.

RSTL

WEE-OO
WEE-OO
WEE-OO
WEE-OO

THOSE AREN'T FAR AWAY.
WHERE ARE THEY COMING FROM?
WEE-OO
WEE-OO

WEE-OO
WEE-OO
WEE-OO
WEE-OO
WEE-OO

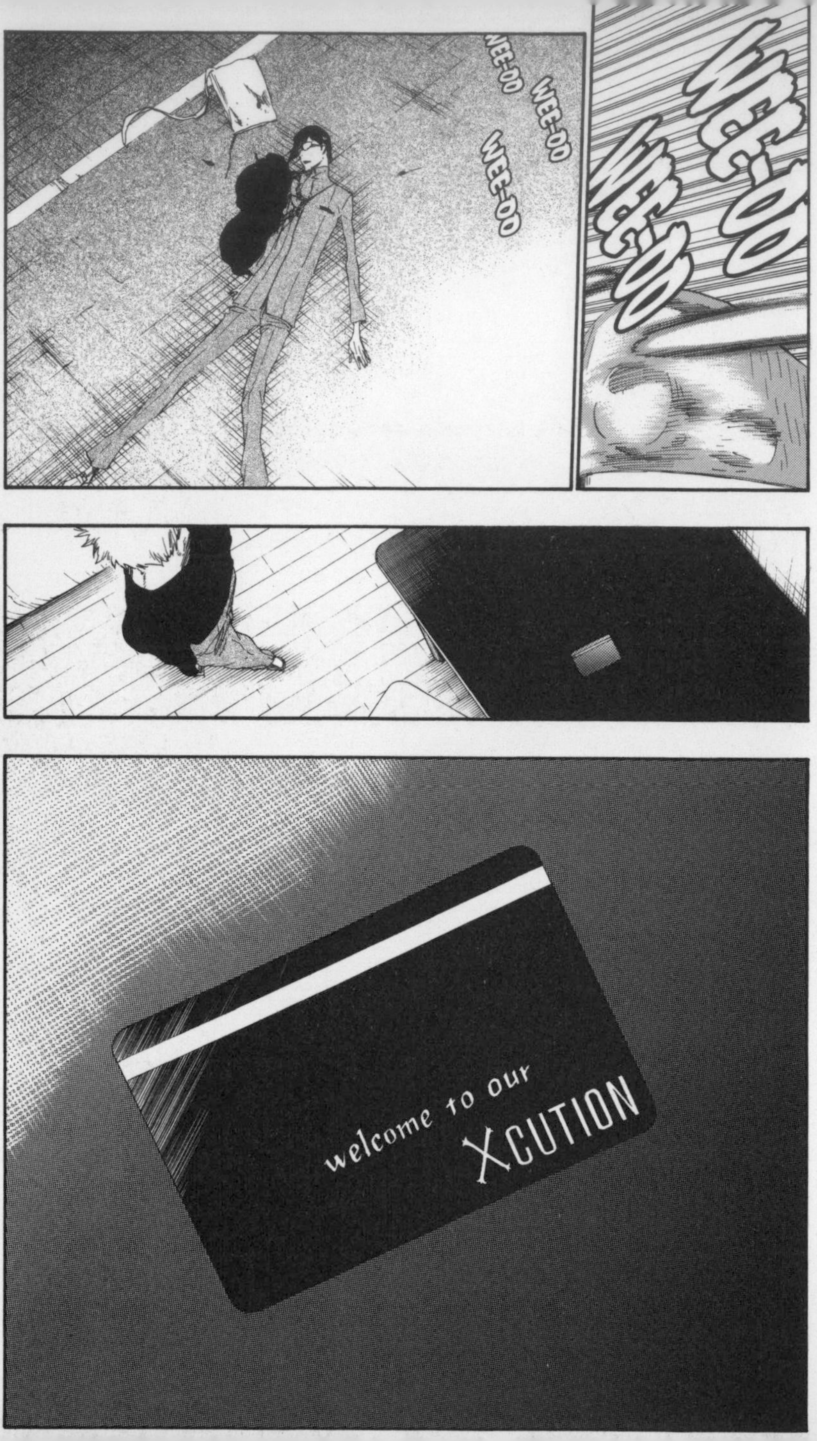

welcome to our
XCUTION

THE NEXT DAY, TEACHER FOUND OUT...
...AND MADE ME SHAVE IT CLEAN OFF, CUE BALL STYLE.
I PLANNED THAT THAT WOULD HAPPEN.

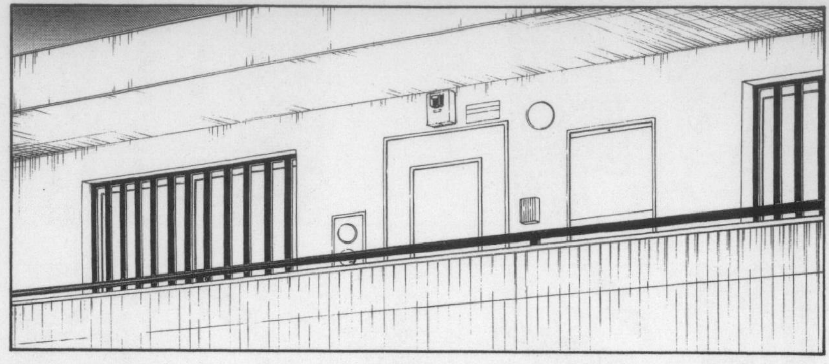

YOU IDIOT!
PHEW~

MY FACE IS STILL RED.
I REALLY ONLY MEANT TO GIVE HIM THE BREAD AND TALK TO HIM AT THE FRONT DOOR.

430. Welcome to our EXECUTION2

SLAM
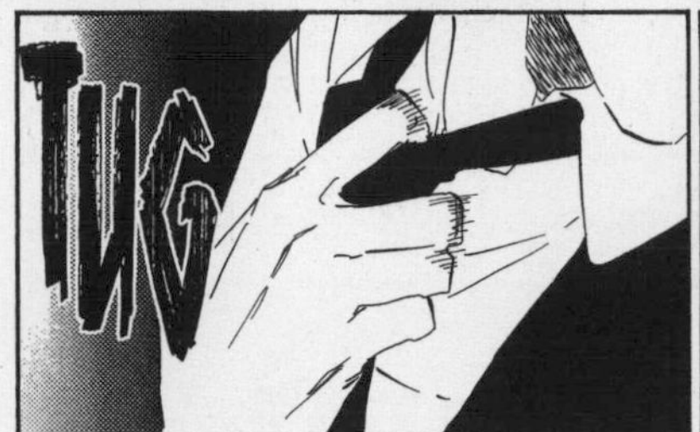
TUG

THUMP

<REALITY>
THADUMP
YOU WANNA COME IN?
I COULDN'T TURN DOWN AN OFFER LIKE THAT!!
SHAKE SHAKE SHAKE

<ORIHIME VISION>
GET IN HERE.

EVEN THOUGH ICHIGO LOVES BREAD SO MUCH, HE TOLD ME TO TAKE SOME HOME WITH ME!
ROLL ROLL ROLL ROLL
HE'S SO NICE!
SO NICE!
S-O N-I-C-E!
ROLL ROLL ROL

N-I-C-E !!
BONK
YOW!
ROLL ROLL ROLL
UH-OH!
CLATTER
GASP!

I...
I'M SORRY, BRO-THER...

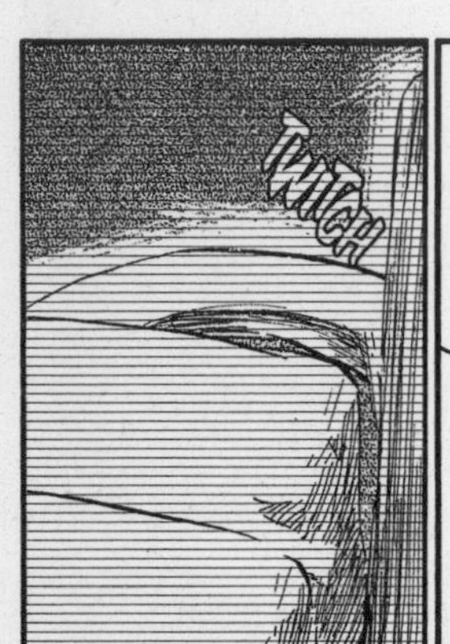
TWITCH

ICHI-GO...
...IS HIDING SOME-THING. I KNOW IT.

IT'S OKAY!
TWITCH

THAT SCARED ME.
WHO'D BE CALLING ME AT THIS HOUR?
STRUM STRUM STRUM
IT'S OKAAAY!
STRUM STRUM STRUM
OH.
IT'S URYU.
IT'S OKAY
STRUM STRUM STRUM
IT'S OKAAAAY!

IT'S OOOOOOKAAAAAAY
BEEP
HELLO?
WHAT'S UP?
HUH?

YES.
UM...
ENRAKU
UOMARO
WHAT?

HUH?

WHERE'S BRO?

UP-STAIRS.
I CALLED HIM, BUT HE SAID HE'LL EAT LATER.

SIIIIGH.
TEENAGE BOYS ARE THE WORST.
SUCH PERVERTS.
KARIN!
PLEASE DON'T SAY INAPPROPRIATE STUFF AT THE TABLE!
AND HE ISN'T LIKE THAT!

SURE, SURE.
LISTEN, YUZU. YOU BETTER DROP THOSE RIDICULOUS NOTIONS YOU HAVE ABOUT OUR BROTHER.
HE'S JUST A TYPICAL BOY.
HE'S NOT SOME ANIME CHARACTER, SO OF COURSE HE'S GONNA—
SLAM

I DON'T THINK THAT ABOUT HIM!!
DASH
HUH?!
OH, I DON'T CARE ANY-MORE!
WAIT! I'M SORRY I MADE FUN OF YOU, YUZU!
COME ON!
I'M DONE TALKING TO YOU!
IT'S YOUR TURN TO CLEAN UP AFTER DINNER ANYWAY, KARIN!
TMP TMP TMP TMP

TMP TMP TMP TMP
SLAM

GREAT ...

I GUESS IT'S BECAUSE ICHIGO WAS COLD TO HER AGAIN.

I'LL HAVE TO MAKE SURE HE COMFORTS HER LATER.

TMP TMP TMP TMP TMP TMP TMP

?

YUZU?

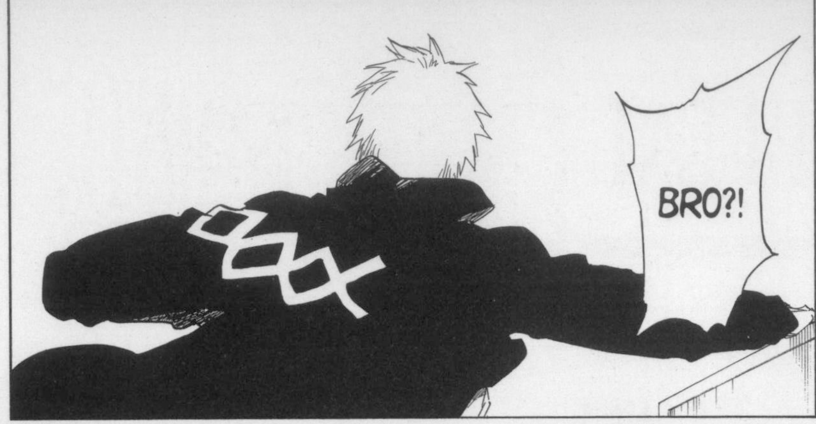
BRO?!

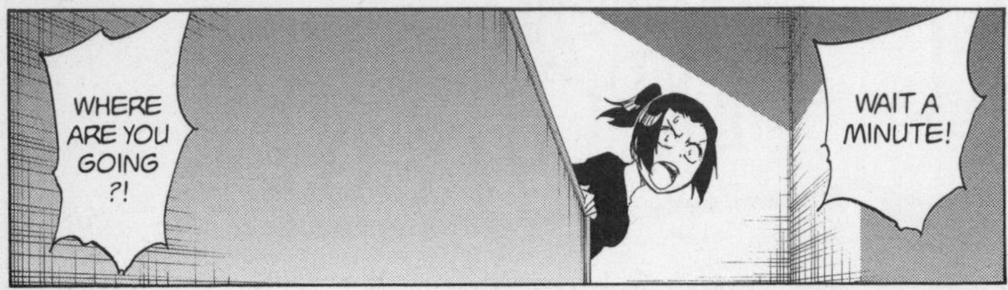
WAIT A MINUTE!
WHERE ARE YOU GOING ?!

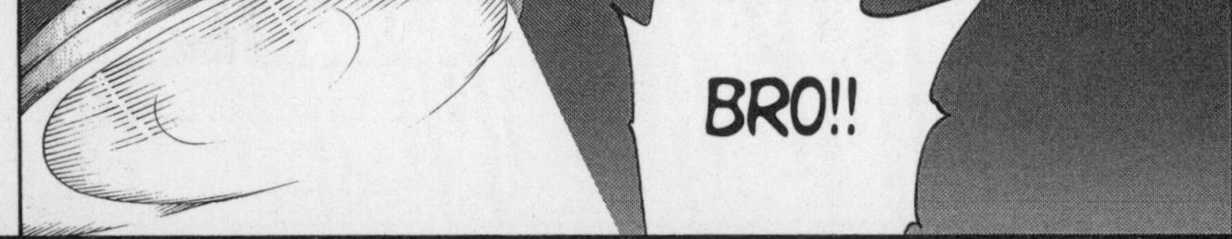
BRO!!

BLEACH

PITAL

430.

AL
Welcome to our
EXECUTION 2

TMP TMP TMP TMP TMP

URYU !!

!

I— ICHIGO!

ORI-HIME!

YOU'RE ALREADY HERE.

WHERE'S CHAD?
HE DIDN'T PICK UP.
I THINK HE'S AT HIS CONSTRUC-TION JOB RIGHT NOW.

DID HE CALL YOU TOO?
SHEESH.
WHAT A BOTHER. I NEVER ASKED HIM TO DO THAT...
URYU...
CLACK

WHAT A BOTHER?

AS ALWAYS, YOU TALK LIKE A GROWN UP. BUT THAT'S ALL.

I THOUGHT I WASN'T SUPPOSED TO HAVE VISITORS.
WHAT IF MY CONDITION WORSENS FROM ALL THESE INTRUDERS BARGING IN?

DON'T BE FOOLISH.
WHO DO YOU THINK PERFORMED THE OPERATION?
YOUR WOUNDS AREN'T GOING TO GET WORSE FROM THIS.

YOU'RE AN AMATEUR WHO GOT SLASHED BY THE ENEMY AND ALMOST DIED.
DON'T YOU DARE GO TELLING THE DOCTOR WHAT HE CAN OR CANNOT DO.

...

READ THIS WAY

HE GOT SLASH-ED?!
WHAT'S HE TALKING ABOUT, URYU?!

IT'S NONE OF YOUR BUSI-NESS.

OF COURSE IT IS!
YOU WERE ATTACKED!
IF YOU COULDN'T HANDLE HIM ON YOUR OWN, THEN WE'VE ALL GOT TO PITCH IN!
SAY SOME-THING!

IT'S IM-PORTANT TO SHARE INFOR-MATION.
DON'T WASTE THE KINDNESS I'VE SHOWN YOU.
YOU BE QUIET!

AWW...
TOO BAD.
HAD YOU RAISED YOUR VOICE ABOUT 5 hz HIGHER, YOU WOULD HAVE REOPENED YOUR WOUNDS.
...

URYU...

I'M SORRY.
ORI-HIME.
THERE REALLY ISN'T ANY-THING I CAN SAY TO YOU RIGHT NOW.
PLEASE GO HOME.

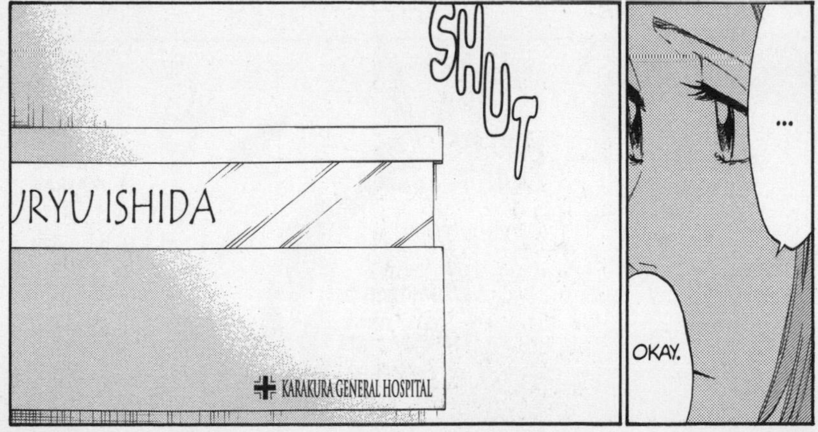
...
OKAY.
SHUT
URYU ISHIDA
KARAKURA GENERAL HOSPITAL

ICHI-
GO...

!
OH... HEY.
YOU MUST BE EX-HAUSTED.
I'LL WALK YOU HOME.
HUH ?!
NO, UH...
ARE YOU SURE?!
GRP

I'LL DRIVE HER HOME.
YOU GET HOME YOUR-SELF.
IF I KEEP YOU OUT TOO LATE, YOUR OLD MAN WILL THROW A FIT.

I UNDER-STAND.
THANK YOU.
OH...

ICHIGO!
I'LL SEE YOU AT SCHOOL TO-MORROW!
HEY.
DON'T YELL SO LOUD IN THE HOS-PITAL.

OH!
I'M SORRY ...
HE DOESN'T SEEM LIKE HE'LL BE MUCH HELP, SO I'LL TELL YOU THIS.
URYU WASN'T ATTACKED BY A HOLLOW.

HUH?
OF COURSE IT WASN'T A SOUL REAPER EITHER.
I STUDIED THE LINGERING SPIRITUAL PRESSURE AROUND HIS CUT...
...AND TO BE FRANK...
...I'M NOT EVEN SURE IF I CAN CALL IT SPIRIT PRESSURE.
IT WAS A SPIRITUAL ENERGY UNLIKE ANYTHING I'VE COME UP AGAINST SO FAR.

READ THIS WAY

WHAT DOES IT MEAN?
DON'T ASK ME.
I'VE ALREADY TOLD YOU EVERYTHING I KNOW.

AND URYU HIMSELF DIDN'T KNOW WHAT HIT HIM.
THAT'S WHY HE DIDN'T TALK TO YOU GUYS.
BECAUSE HE DIDN'T KNOW WHAT TO SAY.
BUT ...

THIS IS JUST MY HYPOTHESIS, BUT...
...THE ENEMY MIGHT HAVE...
...COME INTO POSSESSION OF A POWER WE KNOW NOTHING ABOUT.

BUT THEY ARE HUMAN.

NOT AT ALL LIKE A SOUL REAPER ...

MORE CLOSE TO WHAT...
...YOU AND SADO ARE.

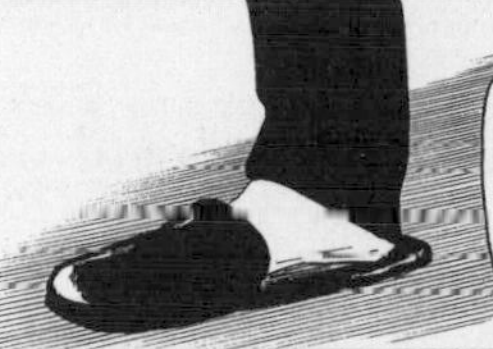
IF I HAD TO SAY, I'D FIT URYU INTO THAT CATEGORY TOO.
IF I WERE TO SUPPOSE THAT THE ATTACK ON URYU WAS AN ATTACK ON HUMANS OF A SIMILAR BREED...

...THEN THE NEXT TO BE ATTACKED...

...IS EITHER YOU OR SADO.

I'LL TAKE YOU HOME NOW.

HUFF!
HUFF!
HUFF!
WHAT'S GOING ON?
DAMMIT!
WHAT HAPPENED RIGHT UNDER MY NOSE?!

ISN'T THERE-

ISN'T THERE ANYTHING I CAN DO ?!

CONCIERGE DESK
TEL: 0120-
BEEP
BEEP
BEEP

HELLO.
YOU'VE REACHED XCUTION.

READ
THIS
WAY

THIS NUMBER ISN'T SHOWING UP IN OUR REGISTRY.
I TAKE IT YOU'RE A NEW MEMBER?
PLEASE STATE YOUR NAME.
ICHI-GO...
...KURO-SAKI.

ICHIGO KUROSAKI, I SEE.
WE'VE BEEN EXPECTING YOU.

WEL-COME...
...TO XCUTION.

IN THE SUMMER OF MY SECOND YEAR, I FINALLY GREW IT OUT.
AND DECIDED TO GET A STYLISH PERM.
OUCH.
YOU'RE LUCKY THE NEW ARC DIDN'T START AROUND THAT TIME.

WELL THEN, MR. ICHIGO KUROSAKI.
PLEASE HANG UP.

HUH?

431. Welcome to our EXECUTION 3

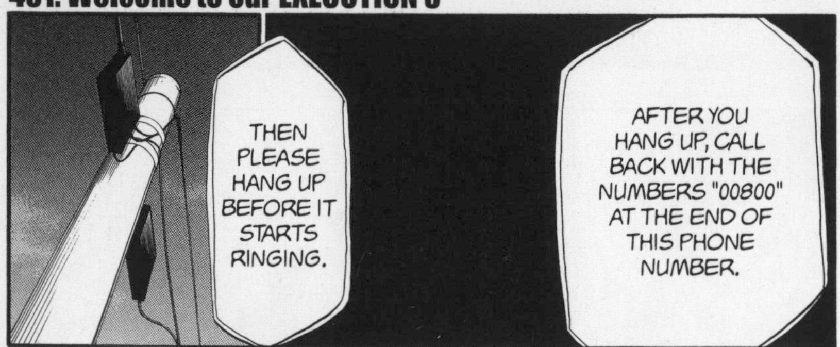
AFTER YOU HANG UP, CALL BACK WITH THE NUMBERS "00800" AT THE END OF THIS PHONE NUMBER.
THEN PLEASE HANG UP BEFORE IT STARTS RINGING.

THEN CALL THAT SAME NUMBER AGAIN...
...AND THEN PLEASE HANG UP AFTER IT RINGS TWICE.
ON THE THIRD CALL...

...YOU WILL BE DIRECTLY CONNECTED TO MR. KUGO GINJO.

CLACK

THAT WAS A REAL PAIN IN THE BUTT.

DON'T SAY THAT.

IF YOU DIDN'T DO THAT, I'D HAVE A LOT MORE TROUBLE.

READ
THIS
WAY

I HAVE TO TALK TO YOU.

I'M SURE.

OTHERWISE, YOU WOULDN'T CALL ME, NOW WOULD YOU?

ICHIGO!!

ICHIGO! DID YOU HEAR ABOUT SADO?

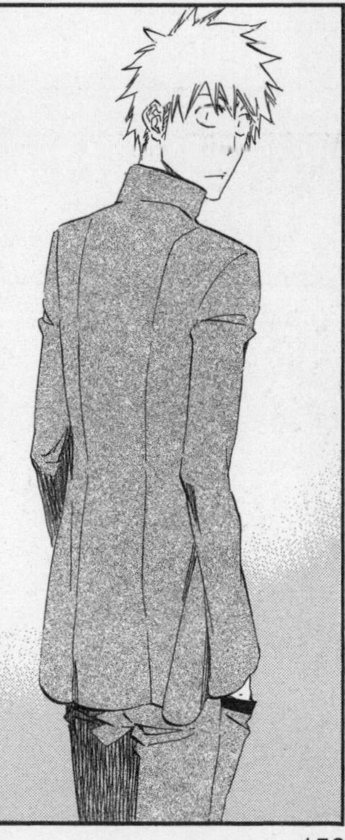

HUH? HEAR ABOUT WHAT?
BE MORE SPECIFIC.
ABOUT WHERE HE IS!

WHERE HE IS ?!
I DUNNO, MAYBE HE CAUGHT A COLD?
OH, DEAR!
SO YOU DON'T KNOW EITHER.
YESTERDAY, I WENT TO HIS CLASS TO TELL HIM ABOUT URYU, BUT...

...IT SEEMS SADO...
...HASN'T BEEN COMING TO SCHOOL LATELY.

I THOUGHT FOR SURE YOU WOULD KNOW SOMETHING ABOUT IT.
BUT I GUESS YOU'RE JUST AS IN THE DARK AS I AM.
I WAS THINKING OF GOING TO CHECK ON HIM AFTER SCHOOL TODAY.

UH... UM...
IF YOU WANT, WE COULD GO TOGETHER...
SORRY.

I'VE GOT STUFF TO DO TODAY.

OH...
S-SURE! I UNDERSTAND! I DIDN'T GIVE YOU MUCH WARNING!
WELL, I'LL GO AND REPORT BACK TO YOU ON HIS CONDITION!
RIGHT.
THANKS.

HAS SOMETHING HAPPENED TO CHAD TOO?

WHAT ON EARTH IS GOING ON HERE?

YOU SORTA SPRANG THIS ON ME LATE IN THE DAY.

READ THIS WAY

HOW'S TO-MORROW WORK FOR YOU?
AT 8 P.M.
MEET ME IN FRONT OF THE OLD APARTMENT BUILDING AT 7-1 CHOBARA IN THE SEVENTH WARD OF NARUKI CITY.

I'LL TALK TO YOU THEN.
DON'T WORRY.

I THINK I CAN HELP YOU OUT.

SCFF

SADO.
HEEEY, SADO. YOOHOOO!

HE'S NOT IN.
IF I WERE TO SUPPOSE THAT THE ATTACK ON URYU WAS AN ATTACK ON HUMANS OF A SIMILAR BREED...
...THEN THE NEXT TO BE ATTACKED...

...IS EITHER YOU...
...OR SADO.

READ THIS WAY

CHILL
SHAKE SHAKE SHAKE
NO NO!
I CAN'T THINK THAT WAY! HE'S FINE!

THERE!
I'LL JUST DO THIS...
RUSTLE RUSTLE
RUSTLE
CLAP CLAP
PLEASE COME BACK TO SCHOOL ALL BETTER TOMORROW!

CLANG CLANG CLANG
HERE'S SOME YUMMY BREAD!
EAT IT AND FEEL BETTER!
-INOUE

19:57

WARD 7 OF CHOBARA DISTRICT IN NARUKI CITY.

CLICK
CLICK
WARD 7...
7...
...!

A DIRTY OLD APARTMENT BUILDING.
THIS MUST BE IT.

YO.

YOU'RE FIVE MINUTES EARLY.
DILI-GENT BOY.

I'M NOT FIVE MINUTES EARLY.
ONLY THREE.

SO.
WHAT DID YOU WANT TO TALK ABOUT?

MY FRIEND WAS ATTACK-ED.

SO?

I WANT YOUR HELP.

FOR A MAN-HUNT?
I THOUGHT YOU DIDN'T TRUST ME.

YOU KNOW ABOUT ME AND MY DAD.
SO YOU CAN'T BE AN ORDINARY HUMAN.

READ THIS WAY

MAYBE.
I STILL DON'T TRUST YOU.
BUT YOU'RE THE ONLY ONE...

YOU MEAN THERE ARE NO OTHER HUMANS...

...YOU CAN TURN TO.

VERY WELL.
FOLLOW ME.

TO BE HONEST, I'D LIKE TO HELP YOU OUT ONLY AFTER YOU TAKE CARE OF MY ORIGINAL REQUEST.

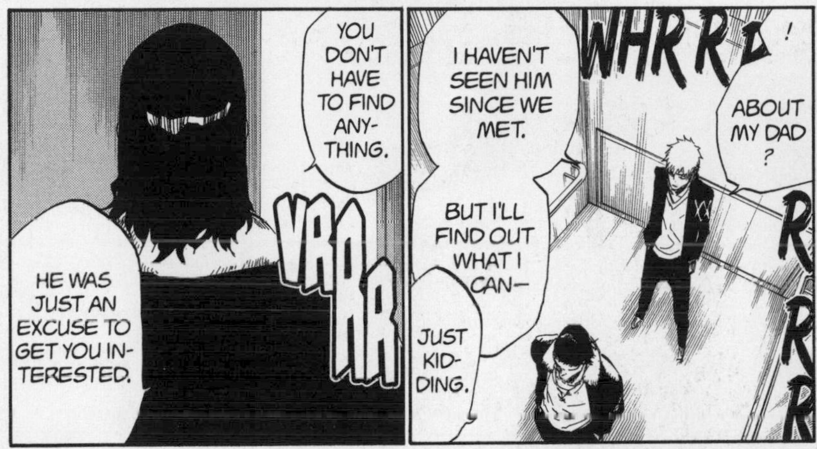
WHRRR!
ABOUT MY DAD?
I HAVEN'T SEEN HIM SINCE WE MET.
BUT I'LL FIND OUT WHAT I CAN—
JUST KIDDING.
RRRR
YOU DON'T HAVE TO FIND ANYTHING.
VRAAR
HE WAS JUST AN EXCUSE TO GET YOU INTERESTED.

AN EXCUSE...?
WE'RE HERE.
WE NEED TO SWIPE THAT CARD.

431.

SWISH

BEEP BEEP BOOP BOOP BOOP

welcome to our EXECUTION

HOW'S THIS UNIT SO BIG?
IT TAKES UP FIVE ROOMS TO THE LEFT AND RIGHT, AND THREE WHOLE FLOORS ABOVE AND BELOW.
SOME OF OUR MEMBERS ARE PRETTY RICH.

READ THIS WAY
NOW THEN.
BEFORE WE GET DOWN TO BUSINESS...
...LET ME TELL YOU ABOUT OUR OBJECTIVE.
OBJECTIVE?
YES.
THE REASON WE'VE APPROACHED YOU.

OUR GOAL...

...IS FOR YOU TO...

...REGAIN YOUR SOUL REAPER POWERS.

IN THE FALL OF MY SECOND YEAR, I LOST MY PERM CUZ IT WAS SO UN-POPULAR...
...AND DYED IT JET-BLACK.
HOLD ON A SECOND.
THIS LITTLE "HAIR UPDATE CORNER" ISN'T ACTUALLY GOING TO CONTINUE, IS IT?

432. The Soul Pantheism

I CANNOT BELIIIIEVE YOU!

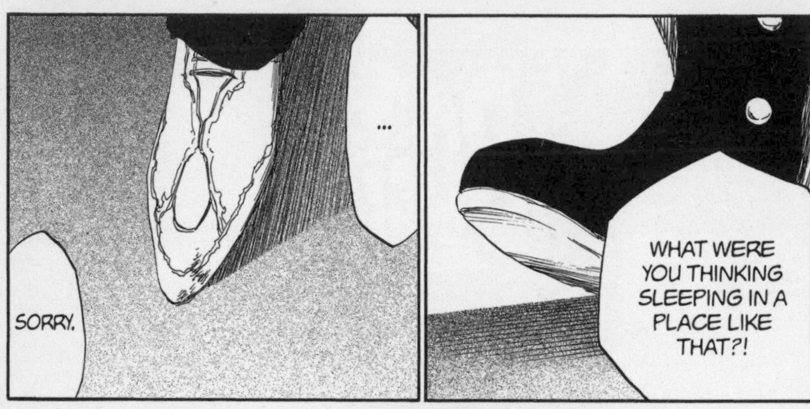
WHAT WERE YOU THINKING SLEEPING IN A PLACE LIKE THAT?!
...
SORRY.

DON'T "SORRY" ME! SHEESH!
DO YOU KNOW WHAT TRACKING YOU DOWN DID TO ME?!
HEY!
NOW THAT I THINK ABOUT IT, WHY DID I HAVE TO TRACK YOU DOWN ANYWAY?!
GINJO SHOULD'VE GONE HIM-SELF!!
RIGHT?!
...

NOW YOU LOOK HERE!
SAY SOMETHING!!
IT'S ALL YOUR FAULT...
...I'M PISSED OFF IN THE FIRST PLACE!!
COME ON!
THERE MUST BE SOMETHING GOING THROUGH THAT HEAD OF YOURS!
OUT WITH IT!
NOTHING.

I'M JUST THINKING HOW YOU TALK ENOUGH FOR TWO PEOPLE.
BONK
OOF!

BLEACH

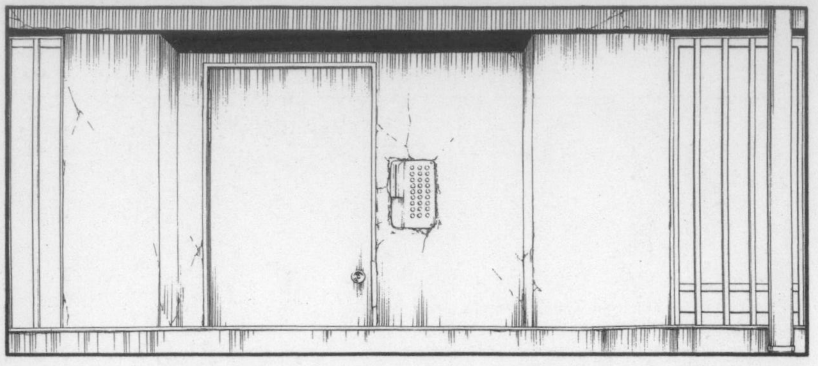

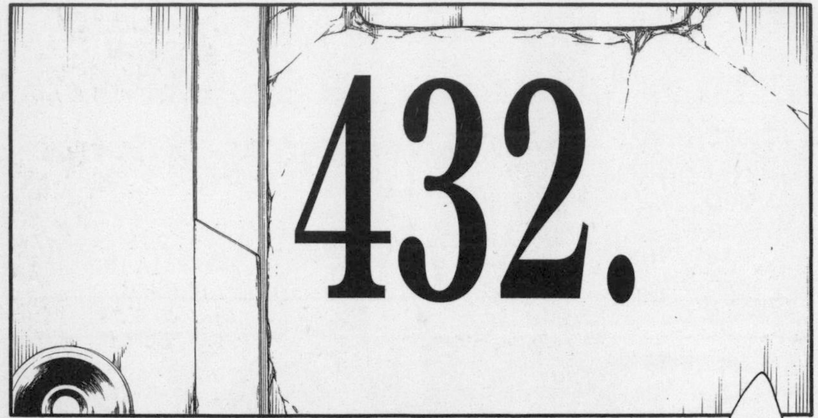

432. The Soul Pantheism

WHAT ?!

WHAT'S THE MATTER?

YOU HEARD ME, DIDN'T YOU?

OUR GOAL...

...IS FOR YOU TO REGAIN YOUR SOUL REAPER POWERS.

THAT'S WHAT I SAID.

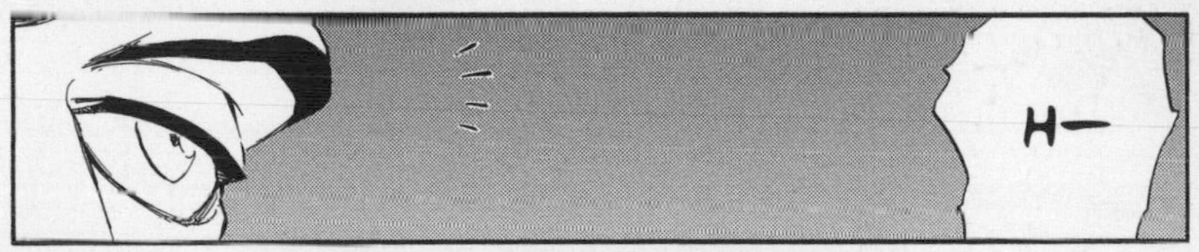
H—

HOW...
HOW CAN I GET THEM BACK?!

AND WHY WOULD YOU EVEN DO THAT FOR ME?!

WHAT ARE YOU REALLY AFTER?!

GRAB

JUST WHO ARE YOU PEOPLE?!

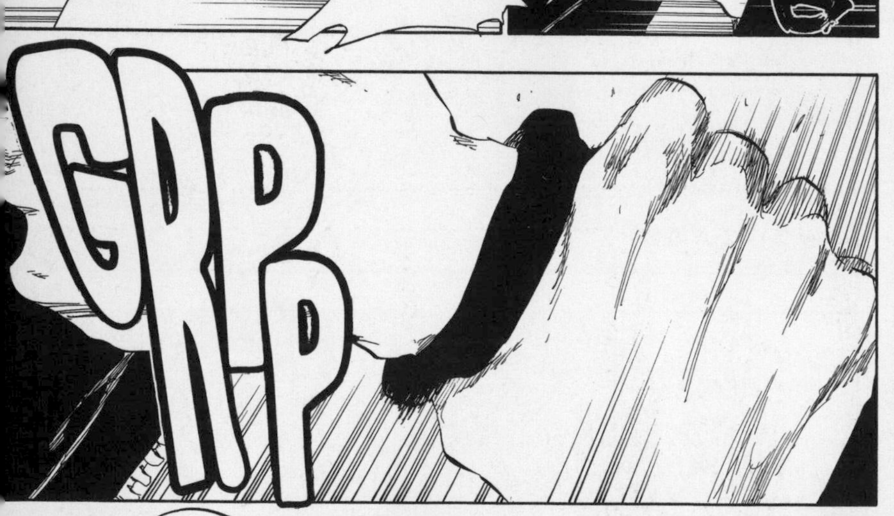
GRP

CALM DOWN.

HOW ABOUT ONE QUESTION AT A TIME?

SIT DOWN.

THE NIGHT'S LONG.

I'LL EXPLAIN IT TO YOU SLOWLY.

CLATTER
YOU WANT ANY-THING TO DRINK?

DON'T LOOK AT ME LIKE THAT.
WE'RE NOT ABOUT TO SERVE ALCOHOL TO A MINOR.
YOU DON'T DRINK, DO YOU?
YOU'RE MORE MORAL THAN YOU LOOK.

ORDER ANYTHING YOU WANT.
WE DON'T HAVE A MENU, BUT WE CARRY THE BASICS.

I DON'T NEED ANY-THING.
FINE THEN.
GET HIM AN ORANGE JUICE.
YES.
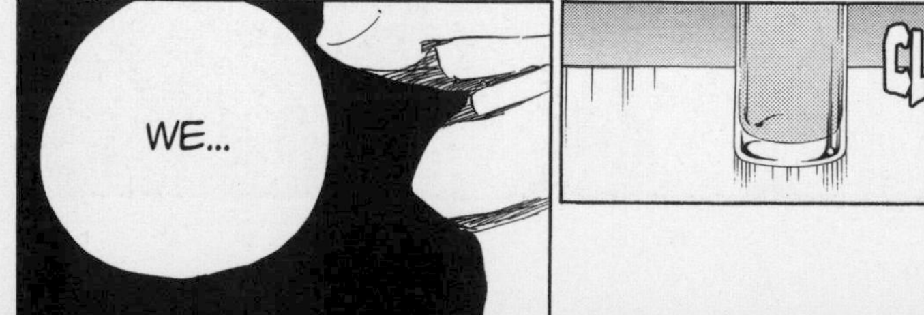
CLACK
WE...

...ARE HUMANS.

OF COURSE, AS YOU SAID BEFORE...
...WE'RE NOT TYPICAL HUMANS.

WE WERE BORN...
...WITH CERTAIN SPECIAL ABILITIES.
SPECIAL ABILITIES?
SHOWING YOU WILL BE THE EASIEST WAY TO EXPLAIN.

WHERE'S THAT LIGHT COMING FROM?

BWOOP

!

SSSLLLIP

GULP

LATTER
JUST NOW...
...I PULLED OUT THE SOUL OF THE ALCOHOL IN THE GLASS AND MADE IT HELP ME DRINK IT.

...
WHAT?!

OUR POWERS...

...ALLOW US TO DRAW OUT THE SOULS THAT RESIDE IN MATERIALS AND PUT THEM TO OUR USE.

THAT FACE TELLS ME YOU DON'T GET WHAT I'M SAYING.
DO YOU THINK ONLY LIVING THINGS HAVE SOULS?

ALL THINGS IN THIS WORLD HAVE SOULS.
NOT JUST CREATURES AND PLANTS.
THE AMOUNT OF SOUL IS SMALL, BUT...
...EVEN TELEPHONE POLES AND CHAIRS AND GLASS HAVE SOULS.

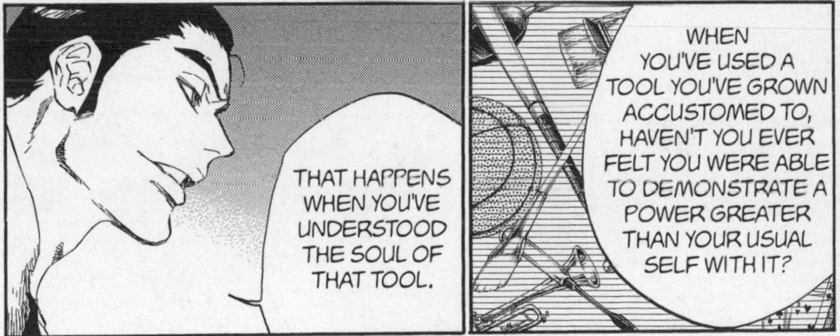
WHEN YOU'VE USED A TOOL YOU'VE GROWN ACCUSTOMED TO, HAVEN'T YOU EVER FELT YOU WERE ABLE TO DEMONSTRATE A POWER GREATER THAN YOUR USUAL SELF WITH IT?
THAT HAPPENS WHEN YOU'VE UNDERSTOOD THE SOUL OF THAT TOOL.

THE SOULS OF THINGS ARE EQUIPPED WITH THE POWER TO HELP THEIR USERS BY NATURE.
OUR POWERS DRAW ON THAT, BOOSTING IT WITH OUR OWN SOULS, TO BE ABLE TO UNLEASH A GREATER POWER.

READ THIS WAY

BY DRAWING OUT THE SOUL IN ASPHALT, IT ASSISTS OUR REPULSION AND ENABLES US TO JUMP HIGHER.

AS FOR LIQUIDS, WE CAN MAKE IT FLY INTO OUR MOUTHS AS YOU JUST SAW.

OR HAVE IT SUPPORT US UNDER OUR FEET SO THAT WE CAN STAND ON WATER.

AND...
...WHEN IT COMES TO A TOOL THAT IS VERY COMPATIBLE WITH US AND THAT WE'VE LEARNED TO MASTER...
...WE CAN CHANGE ITS VERY FORM.

FOR EXAMPLE...
IN MY CASE, IT'S THIS NECKLACE.

WATCH.
WHOOSH

CHOOM

WHA...

THIS IS WHAT I'M TALKING ABOUT.

WE CALL THIS ABILITY...
...FULL-BRING.
KLATCH

BAM

I'M HOME!

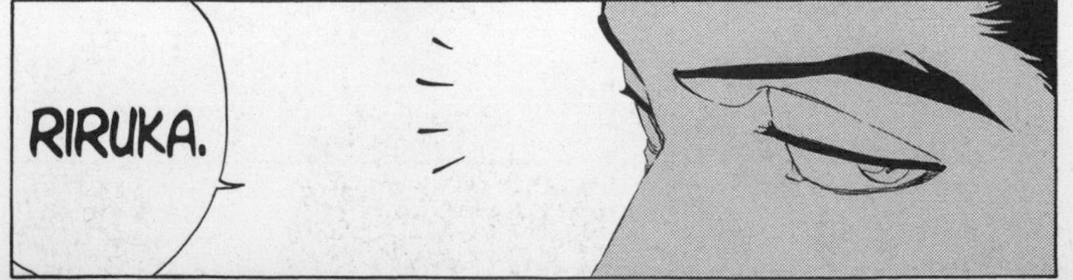

YOU'RE BACK SOONER THAN I EXPECTED.
DID YOU FIND HIM?
I SURE DID!
THAT SHINY THING IS YOUR SWORD, ISN'T IT? WHY'D YOU BRING IT OUT, IDIOT!

IT'S TOO DARK IN HERE!
GET SOME LIGHTS INSTALLED. I CAN'T SEE A THING!
WE HAVE NO PLANS TO INSTALL ANY LIGHTS.
WEAR YOUR GLASSES IF YOU HAVE TO SEE.

I HATE MY GLASS-ES!
AND MY CONTACTS EVEN MORE!

THEY DRY MY EYES OUT BECAUSE MY EYES ARE SO BIG AND PRETTY!
WE'RE NOT LISTEN-ING.

WHO'S SHE?
RIRUKA DOKU-GAMINE.
AN ALLY.

WHAT?! AND WHO'S THAT SITTING THERE ?!
HMMMM!
I'LL INTRODUCE HIM LATER.
COME IN ALREADY.

DON'T GO BOSSING ME AROUND!

COME ON!
GET YOUR BUTT IN HERE!

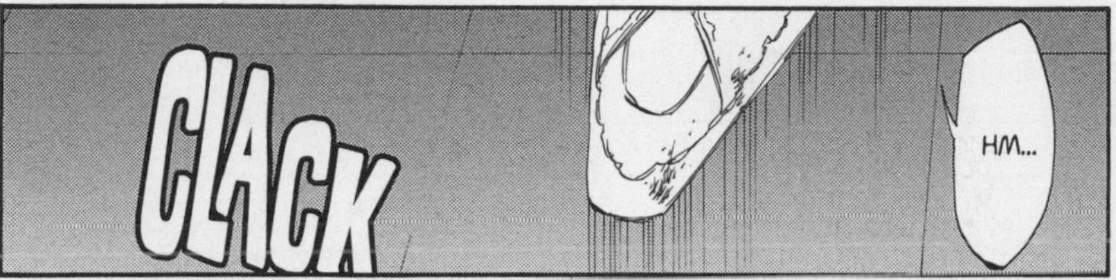
HM...
CLACK

CLACK

WHA...

CHAD...!

Next Volume

When Ichigo learns the goals of the Fullbringers, he'll have to decide whether or not he should help them. Meanwhile, a dark shadow approaches Orihime...!

Coming soon!